Peter Baelz is Canon of Christ Church and Regius Professor of
Moral and Pastoral Theology in the University of Oxford.

THE FORGOTTEN DREAM

THE
FORGOTTEN
DREAM

Experience, Hope and God

Bampton Lectures for 1974

PETER BAELZ

*Canon of Christ Church and Regius Professor
of Moral and Pastoral Theology*

MOWBRAYS
LONDON & OXFORD

CBPac

© Peter Baelz, 1975
ISBN 0 264 66200 8
First published 1975
by A. R. Mowbray & Co Ltd
The Alden Press, Osney Mead
Oxford, OX2 0EG

Text set in 11 on 13pt Times Roman

Photoset, printed and bound
in Great Britain by
REDWOOD BURN LIMITED
Trowbridge & Esher

CONTENTS

And the king said to them, 'I had a dream, and my spirit is troubled to know the dream.' Then the Chaldeans said to the king, 'O king, live for ever! Tell your servants the dream, and we will show the interpretation'. . . . The king answered, 'I know with certainty that you are trying to gain time, because you see that the word from me is sure that if you do not make the dream known to me, there is but one sentence for you. You have agreed to speak lying and corrupt words before me till the times change. Therefore tell me the dream, and I shall know that you can show me its interpretation.' The Chaldeans answered the king, 'There is not a man on earth who can meet the king's demand; for no great and powerful king has asked such a thing of any magician or enchanter or Chaldean. The thing that the king asks is difficult, and none can show it to the king except the gods, whose dwelling is not with flesh.'

Dan. 2.3,4,8–11

PREFACE

I have attempted in these lectures, which are here printed in much the same shape as they were delivered Sunday by Sunday in the University Church of St Mary the Virgin, not to establish a position but to explore a predicament.

The predicament is that of 'would-be Christians' who find themselves caught between the opposing fires of belief and unbelief. To their dismay the line of fire seems to go right through the centre of their own minds and hearts.

Anyone who is unable to understand such a predicament, whether in himself or in another, will discover little or nothing of value in what follows and is advised to read no further.

Anyone who understands this predicament only too well, but looks for some safe conduct which will remove him once and for all from the line of fire, would also be wise to read no further. No safe conduct is offered him. One could say that the lectures end roughly where they began.

I hope, however, that there may be some who in reading these lectures will acquire a deeper insight into the nature of their predicament and be released from the fearful immobility which threatens to root them to the spot.

I am concerned, therefore, less with the specific contents of Christian belief than with the grounds for such belief.

Theologians often argue a case and defend a doctrine. However cogent their arguments they sometimes fail to convince, simply because the presuppositions from which they argue are not shared by the reader, who stands in a different place from the one where they stand. He, very naturally, wishes to start the discussion from where he is, not from where they are.

In moral theology a distinction is sometimes drawn between the approach of the moral theologian and that of the moral counsellor. The former is said to be concerned with the determination of the moral law, the latter with the development and growth of the individual person's own conscientious judgement. This distinction, which is applied to action, can, I suggest, be analogously applied to belief. It is sometimes more important that a person be enabled to appropriate belief for himself than that he be informed of accepted doctrines.

My approach, then, to the exploration of the predicament of the 'would-be Christian' represents a kind of pastoral theology. Although the argument is as lucid and as tight as I can make it, it aims at understanding rather than assent. My method is reflective rather than apologetic. I do not wish to imply by this that I consider the task of the systematic theologian unimportant; far from it. But to each task its own time and place.

It was hardly reasonable of Nebuchadnezzar to ask his wise men not only to interpret his dream for him but also to tell him what it was that he had dreamed. But he had a reason for his request. His spirit was troubled. He had forgotten the dream. The dream, however, had not 'forgotten' him.

I do not pretend that there is anything new or profound in what I have to say. My indebtedness to others will be obvious on every page. I should, however, like to acknowledge a special debt of gratitude to those who, through their writings or their friendship, have taught me the little that I understand of hope and God—and not least to my wife, who has 'walked along the way with me' with love, patience and laughter.

The superscript numbers refer to Notes, on pp. 143-8.

EXTRACT
FROM THE LAST WILL AND TESTAMENT
OF THE LATE
REV. JOHN BAMPTON
Canon of Salisbury

'. . . I give and bequeath my Lands and Estates to the Chancellor, Masters, and Scholars of the University of Oxford for ever, to have and to hold all and singular the said Lands or Estates upon trust, and to the intents and purposes hereinafter mentioned; that is to say, I will and appoint that the Vice-Chancellor of the University of Oxford for the time being shall take and receive all the rents, issues, and profits thereof, and (after all taxes, reparations, and necessary deductions made) that he pay all the remainder to the endowment of eight Divinity Lecture Sermons, to be established for ever in the said University, and to be performed in the following:

'I direct and appoint, that, upon the first Tuesday in Easter Term, a Lecturer be yearly chosen by the Heads of Colleges only, and by no others, in the room adjoining to the Printing-House, between the hours of ten in the morning and two in the afternoon, to preach eight Divinity Lecture Sermons, the year following, at St. Mary's in Oxford, between the commencement of the last month in Lent Term, and the end of the third week in Act Term.

'Also I direct and appoint, that the eight Divinity Lecture Sermons shall be preached upon either of the following Subjects—to conform and establish the Christian Faith, and to confute all heretics and schismatics—upon the divine authority of the holy Scriptures—upon the authority of the writings of the primitive Fathers, as to the faith and practice of the primitive Church—upon the Divinity of our Lord and Saviour Jesus Christ—upon the Divinity of the Holy Ghost—upon the Articles of the Christian Faith, as comprehended in the Apostles' and Nicene Creeds.

'Also I direct, that thirty copies of the eight Divinity Lecture Sermons shall be always printed, within two months after they are preached; and one copy shall be given to the Chancellor of the University, and one copy to the Head of every College, and one copy to the Mayor of the city of Oxford, and one copy to be put into the Bodleian Library; and the expense of printing them shall be paid out of the revenue of the Land or Estates given for establishing the Divinity Lecture Sermons; and the Preacher shall not be paid nor be entitled to the revenue, before they are printed.

'Also I direct and appoint, that no person shall be qualified to preach the Divinity Lecture Sermons, unless he has taken the degree of Master of Arts at least, in one of the two Universities of Oxford or Cambridge; and that the same person shall never preach the Divinity Lecture Sermons twice.'

1

APPEAL TO EXPERIENCE

'I believe; help my unbelief!'   (Mark 9.24)

In a former age John Bampton, Prebendary of Salisbury, directed in his will that a lecturer be appointed 'to preach eight Divinity Lecture Sermons'. But what sort of performance is a Lecture Sermon? The phrase itself sounds an uncertain note in our twentieth-century ears. It conjures up the suspicion of a paradox. Is not a sermon the exposition of a word of God, proclaimed from the standing pulpit of a received and authoritative faith? And is not a lecture the utterance of a word of man, delivered from a moving point of inquiry and doubt? Can sermon and lecture become one without confusion of natures?

Bampton's own intentions were clear and precise. The purpose of these Lecture Sermons was 'to confirm and establish the Christian Faith, and to confute all heretics and schismatics'. A clarion call to do battle for truth and God! However, for better or worse times and manners, even theological manners, have changed. The lines between orthodoxy and heresy, church and schism, even between belief and unbelief, are no longer to be drawn as confidently or as definitively as once they were. This being the case, along with any attempt to confirm the Christian faith, if not actually prior to it, there must go a renewed effort to understand that faith. It is to this basic task that I shall in the main devote myself. I hope, therefore, that had our benefactor been alive today, he would have countenanced and approved an interpretation of his wishes which, while in no way detracting from his central concern with the substance of Christian faith, nevertheless adopts an approach which is exploratory rather than declamatory and a method which is cautiously reflective rather than bravely apologetic. Such method and approach have not been adopted arbitrarily. For myself, I confess, I can do no other.

In all that follows I shall have in mind a certain type of person. Such a one finds himself more often than not inhabiting a strange, bewildering and uncomfortable no-man's land between belief and unbelief. Let us borrow a term from Professor Price's Gifford Lectures and call this person a 'half-believer'. As Price himself points out, half-believers are not to be confused with lukewarm believers or with believers-in-half. They are no modern Laodiceans, whose life and practice belie their formal expression of faith. Hypocrisy is not a charge which can with justice be levelled against them, as it might surely be levelled against someone, say, professing to pursue a middle course between honesty and dishonesty. In fact honesty and integrity exercise on their minds an unquestioned and unquestionable, even a passionate, claim. A concern for truthfulness, in belief and action, is one of their few remaining absolutes. Nor is it the case that they give their full assent to half the Christian creed, while refusing assent to the other half. Certainly there are items of belief, which have been held by most Christians in the past, and which are still held by some in the present, but which they themselves feel obliged to reject. This, however, is not the source of their particular dilemma. They recognise the fact that the thematic articulation of Christian faith is inevitably a changing and developing process, in part dependent on developments in knowledge and variations in culture. In order to say the same thing in one age as was said in another age it may become necessary to say a different thing. The one gospel of Jesus Christ, the same yesterday, today and for ever, will find differing expressions in differing contexts. Old and new are symbiotic. Nevertheless, despite such undeniable and inevitable change, they cannot help thinking that there must surely be some underlying and integrating unity of vision and belief, of pattern and structure, to which it may never be possible to give a precise and final expression, but which nevertheless exercises a control on the range of possible expressions and prevents arbitrary and haphazard variations. In some sense or other the whole Christian thing must hang together, whatever that thing may be. Christians should at least possess a family likeness, such as to distinguish them from members of other families. The suggestion that they should pick out from the tradition the bits and pieces which happen to fit their own opinions and preferences, and straightway jettison the rest as so much superfluous freight, seems to smack of superficiality, if not of dishonesty. To their way of thinking it is unlikely that such bits and pieces will make a coherent picture on their own, or that they can be readily combined with other bits and pieces borrowed from other creeds and systems. Paradoxically, a kind of all-or-nothing hovers around and characterises their half-belief, leaving them painfully dissatisfied with the condition in which they find themselves and from which they do not know how to escape. They believe and do not believe at one and the same time—or, if such a condition defies the canons of logical propriety, at successive and unpredictably alternating times. They are divided within themselves. They have double vision.

It cannot be said that they simply go with the crowd and take on the colours of their companions. Of course the opinions and examples of others weigh with them. They are as open as other men to the influence of the company they keep. Sometimes, it is true, they feel the appeal of belief when they are with believers and of unbelief when they are with unbelievers. But it is not always so. It may happen that, when they are in the company of militant, self-styled 'true' believers, they find themselves moving towards unbelief; and again that when they are in the company of equally militant, self-styled 'rational' unbelievers, they find themselves moving towards belief. In fact, however, their outlooks and attitudes are not at the mercy of any group. They are intensely their own. Seeds both of belief and of unbelief are lodged in their souls, but no single, pure blossom either of faith or of scepticism comes to full flower.

The 'true believer' may rebuke them for their lack of faith. Half-belief, he tells them, is only a sophisticated name for unbelief. A genuine believer must be certain of his belief. He must know. Where this certainty is lacking, there can be only opinion or unbelief. They must confess that at the root of their temptation to unbelief lie sins of intellectual arrogance and pride. They must make an act of penitence and faith, commit themselves unreservedly to God, say their prayers and forget their doubts. Difficulties, practical and theoretical, there may be, but doubt never. For doubt is more than temptation. It is sin, and leads away from God.

Despite, however, such powerful exhortation the half-believer is not to be bludgeoned into belief. The advice, he admits, is well-intended. Sinner he may be. Certainly he, like other men, has much of which to be ashamed. If God there be, he is not to be numbered among God's most obedient and loyal servants. Nevertheless, his half-belief persists. Faith and understanding cannot be so simply divorced. Difficulties tend to turn into doubts. He might supposedly get rid of both in something like the manner of David Hume's recommended cure for radical philosophic doubt—carelessness and inattention, involvement in the occupations of common life, or even a game of backgam- mon. But once these difficulties and doubts have seriously engaged his heart and mind, in a spirit totally different from one of destructive cynicism, can he honestly abandon him- self to a game of religious backgammon, so shifting his diffi- culties and doubts from the centre of his consciousness that they become repressed in his unconscious and in that dangerous way 'forgotten'?

The 'rational unbeliever' may rebuke them for their cre- dulity and superstition, their childish fancies and their flight from freedom, and demand that they spell out their beliefs clearly and distinctly and justify them at the bar of reason.

Again, this is well-intended advice. The half-believer is no enemy to reason. He will have a reasonable faith or none at all. He is himself well aware of the propensity of the human heart to escape from the stringent demands of the real world into a fantasy world of make-believe. The state of half- belief, he is the first to admit, is the result of internal strife, the sign of a divided personality. It may be the case that one of the warring parties within is the helpless but would-be omnipotent child which has never grown up. What if he has yet to learn how to put away childish things? However, he is not fully persuaded by this psychological diagnosis. There are aspects of his experience and reflection which cause him to doubt the final urgency of the sceptic's arguments.

5

Neither the sceptic's view of what constitutes the 'real world', nor his definition of the criteria of 'reasonable belief', is beyond dispute. Although he himself might be hard-pressed to present a convincing case for belief in God, he is not yet fully persuaded that no such case exists or could exist. It would certainly be no simple, knock-down affair. It would be in terms neither of logical necessity nor of statistical probability. It would have to be complex and cumulative. Like any other large-scale, comprehensive metaphysical theory it would have to be assessed in terms of its internal consistency and coherence, and of its power to illuminate and integrate the full range of human experience and understanding. Reasons advanced for and against would depend for their validity as much on judgement as on argumentation, and the exact weight to be given to any particular judgement could not be reduced to rule or calculated on an agreed scale. It does not follow that in venturing into this area reason has exceeded its proper limits, or that one large-scale metaphysical belief is as good—or as bad—as another. Judgements do not become arbitrary at the point at which they cannot be reduced to rules. It does, however, seem to follow that the debate between belief and unbelief, things being as they are, is likely to remain inconclusive. There will be diverse and conflicting judgements. This fact in itself might be taken as an additional argument for not believing, or at least for suspending belief. However, we are not dealing here with a matter for detached speculation. Belief and unbelief are intimately connected with the way in which a man lives his life and shapes his world. A choice cannot be evaded. To suspend belief at this point is itself a movement towards unbelief. Practice has a certain priority over theory. If on theoretical grounds the half-believer constantly finds the scales tilting towards unbelief, it is not because he finds that unbelievers are in general and on the whole more reasonable people than believers, but because the believer, in seeking to extend the area of reasonable assertion beyond that which is shared by himself and unbeliever alike, sets out to occupy a larger and less tractable ground. Consequently, his position is more exposed and more vulnerable than that of his antagonist. He has ventured beyond the bounds of intellectual security. He has put himself at risk.

One final point in our impressionistic sketch of the half-believer. Belief and unbelief exercise a claim on his allegiance in the sphere of action as well as in the sphere of thought. Because, concretely considered, religion is a total way of life in which belief and action are significantly interwoven, he adopts as one of his criteria of judgement the fruitfulness of faith in the lives and characters of those who espouse it. He may be uncertain of the precise relation of belief to action; whether, for example, religious beliefs are simply psychological aids to moral endeavour, engaging the imagination and inspiring the will, or whether they penetrate more deeply into the very nature and character of action itself. In either case, however, their value, if not their validity, can in part be determined by the quality of the action to which they give rise and the character of the life in which they find fulfilment. Let the tree, then, be judged by its fruits. When, however, he tries to use this criterion in order to judge between the respective fruits of belief and unbelief, he is apt to find his half-belief confirmed rather than dissipated. It is not that he attempts the virtually impossible task of comparing the histories of belief and unbelief, and then of drawing up accounts of the social goods and evils effected in the name of either. It is rather that he discovers his saints, models of what to his mind human life

ideally ought to embody, among both believers and unbelievers. Neither group has the monopoly of human virtues and
graces. Integrity, compassion, self-forgetfulness, love, and
numerous other expressions of beauty, truth and goodness,
he finds now here, now there. Are there, then, no distinctive
fruits of belief and unbelief? Perhaps there are; but they are
difficult to isolate, and still more difficult to describe. Suppose, however, that he singles out, albeit with hesitation, a
certain deep acceptance of life, a responsive obedience, in
his saint of belief who walks humbly with his God, and a
certain passionate protest, a radical discontent, in his saint
of unbelief who strives in the company of his fellow-men to
erect a human habitation in an indifferent universe, he finds
himself acknowledging a profound if paradoxical admiration for both kinds of sanctity. So the inner debate continues.

The ground which the half-believer occupies does not
provide him with a stable resting-place. He does not relish
his position. The division within himself is painful, if not
absurd. It is also potentially destructive. Can a kingdom
divided against itself stand? Integrity demands that he continue faithful to the limited and conflicting insights which he
already has. The temptation to run for safety to the
entrenched position of belief or unbelief is to be resisted.
However, his instinct for the unity of truth and his search
for personal identity inform him that he inhabits no abiding
city. He must be on the move. But in what direction? If the
move is not to be settled by chance and circumstance, or determined by the blind forces of cultural change, he must
have a hand in it himself. He must explore the terrain and
seek a path through the minefields, wherever it may lead
him in the end. For this purpose he requires a compass and,
if possible, some sort of a map—a compass to give him his

bearings and a map to give him an idea of his surroundings. What is by the very nature of the case unavailable to him is a detailed itinerary with the stages of his journey and his final destination carefully planned and pre-arranged.

So much by way of a sketch of our contemporary half-believer. If there is in fact no such person, and I have only dreamed him up, then there is nothing more that can usefully be said. Even if you recognise the character, either in yourself or in some other, but regard it as the expression of a sick soul, a case to be sent to the preacher to be saved from sin or to the psychiatrist to be cured of neurosis, then it is unlikely that you will have much time for the reflections which follow. For my contention is that neither preaching nor psychiatry, excellent as these practices may be, will by themselves meet the half-believer's needs. What he needs, first and foremost, is a deeper understanding of himself and his situation. To attempt to contribute to such understanding will be our remaining task.

The culture shared by believer and unbeliever in the West today has been in large part shaped by the enormous successes of the natural sciences and their technological off-shoots. We possess an ever-increasing knowledge of the world in which we live, the kind of knowledge which extends the range of our power to plan and to act. If there is a noise in the water-pipes, we send for the plumber rather than the psalmist, and at the back of the plumber's craft lies the massive support of the science of engineering.

The authority of our scientific knowledge does not lie in itself. It is no mere 'given', coming to us out of the past and to be accepted in the present without cavil or question. It is a developing human construct. Explanations and theories are to be discarded if and when better explanations and theories are forthcoming. When changes occur, radical changes included, there is no sudden failure of scientific nerve. Underlying scientific beliefs there is a still more sure confidence in scientific approach and method.

> There are a steadily increasing number of persons [wrote John Dewey] who find security in *methods* of inquiry, of observation, experiment, of forming and following working hypotheses. Such persons are not unsettled by the upsetting of any special belief, because they retain security of procedure. They can say, borrowing language from another context, though this method slay my most cherished beliefs, yet will I trust it. . . . The guardianship of truth seems to them to have passed over to the *method* of attaining and attesting beliefs. In this latter fundamental they rest in intellectual and emotional peace. . . .[1]

It is no doubt possible to exaggerate the unity of scientific method. There is no single, specific method of investigation which is identical in all the various sciences. Nevertheless, there is surely a unity of approach and expectation. We may express this in the words of another writer:

> It is the discovery that discoveries can be made, rather than any particular theory or even any particular method, which lies at the root of the great revolution in our lives— one of the few irreversible changes in the history of man, which we associate with the name of science.[2]

'The discovery that discoveries can be made.' We can in principle find out for ourselves. We do not have to depend on the unquestioned and unquestionable assertions of others. We can put an opinion or a theory to the test; we do not have to accept or reject it without further ado. We can appeal to experience and experiment.

Of course, it is important not to over-call one's hand.

First, it is necessary to recognise the proper place of authority even in the pursuit of science. No-one has the time, the ability or the facilities for testing every scientific assertion. There must always be an element of trust in the integrity and standards of the scientific community in which one participates. Without such trust there would be no progress. Even so, such trust is conditional, not absolute. It may be called into question and put to the test. It is always possible for further investigation to expose a Piltdown man or a Vinland map.

Secondly, scientific theories go well beyond anything which might properly be called 'experience'. They cannot be conclusively confirmed, nor indeed in every case conclusively refuted, by any incontrovertible appeal to experience. Of course, to be tenable they have to 'fit the facts'. But neither 'fit' nor 'fact' is a completely determinate concept. The fit may be more or less comfortable; it need not be skin-tight. And the facts do not present themselves to the observer as a set of ready-made objects, like so many articles on a tray. What is to count as a fact will in part depend on the scientific theories which are being presupposed, and awkward 'facts' may sometimes be discounted as freak and unreliable or ignored as inexplicable.

However, when all proper qualifications have been made, it still remains the case that an appeal to experience, to careful observation and experiment, lies at the heart of scientific procedures and colours a science-orientated culture. The links between the most abstruse scientific theories and everyday experience may be subtle and extended. Nevertheless, the links are there and can be shown to be there.

It is the variety of largely independent scientific theories, which may be independently appealed to in certifying empirical secular methods, that makes a scientist's, or everyday observer's, claims to knowledge so convincing. And most of all, there is the deliberate linking of all scientific perceptions and assessments to everyday perception, the seeing, hearing and touching of plain and barely mistakable everyday things. However much science goes beyond this, it must include and explain what cannot but command the assent of the least scientific.[3]

Such an experiential grounding of our claims to knowledge of the world around us has become part and parcel of our cultural identity. It is not surprising, therefore, that we should wish to adopt a similar approach in understanding and testing our religious beliefs. If these beliefs are other than a set of pseudo-scientific theories, reflecting an illegitimate extrapolation of the methods of scientific explanation into a dark region where such explanation no longer obtains, and if they are not simply to be accepted or rejected as self-accrediting dogmas, given, ultimate and beyond all reason, then some kind of appeal to experience, whatever its precise shape and form, must be allowed. Nor is religion itself hostile to such an appeal to experience. It proclaims a gospel, offers a way of salvation and suggests a practice. 'Taste and see how gracious the Lord is.' 'They that wait upon the Lord shall renew their strength, they shall mount up with wings as eagles, they shall run and not be weary, they shall walk and not faint.' Is there, then, underlying and offering a test of religious beliefs something analogous to the everyday perception of things and persons which under-lies and offers a test of scientific beliefs? Is there a kind of religious perception? Is there, indeed, a perception of God?

There are some believers who would claim to have just

such a perception, whether they call it a sense of the presence of God or an encounter with the reality of God. Furthermore, they would say that they were as sure of the divine being which they perceived as you or I might be sure of the bus edging its way past us in the High or of the young lady sitting at the cash-desk in Sainsbury's. They do not merely know about God, they know God. 'To the believer faith is not a probability but a certainty.'[4]

To such as the Old Testament prophets and New Testament apostles God was:

> a sheer given reality, as inescapably to be reckoned with as destructive storm and life-giving sunshine, or the fixed contours of the land, or the hatred of their enemies and the friendship of their neighbours. The biblical writers were (sometimes, though doubtless not at all times) as vividly conscious of being in God's presence as they were of being in a material environment.[5]

Have we here instances of a kind of religious perception, of a direct awareness of God? So indeed it might be claimed on behalf of the giants of the Judaeo-Christian tradition; and so too, I think, it would be quietly but confidently claimed by a not inconsiderable number of more ordinary believers.

There is no need to reject this claim out of hand—unless one has already and arbitrarily restricted the range of human awareness, for example, to sense impressions, or physical objects, and maintains that all else is a logical construction out of these basic data and consequently nothing of which one can be directly aware. On the other hand, the claim to be directly aware of God can be reasonably doubted, in a way in which the claim to be directly aware of a material environment cannot be reasonably doubted. It is impossible to say that the perceived existence of God cannot but command the assent of the least religious. Alternative interpretations of the experience can be presented and plausibly argued. Since this is so, however convinced the believer himself may be that he is aware of God, and granted even the possibility that he is in fact aware of God, nevertheless, when others equally as reasonable as himself dispute the truth of his claim, he is bound to admit that it is possible that he is mistaken and should be prepared, if he has the requisite ability, to argue in the context of a supporting theory that he is not mistaken.[6]

Religious experiences, to speak now in general terms, are notoriously ambiguous. They permit of atheistic as well as of theistic interpretations. Even if we distinguish sharply between two irreducible kinds of religious experience (the mystical and the numinous), and stress the sense of overwhelming otherness that characterises the latter, so rendering it a likely vehicle for belief in God, it still remains uncertain whether such numinous experience is not equally plausibly susceptible to an interpretation in naturalistic terms. The sheer power and otherness of the sea, for example, may affect a man with an overwhelming sense of a fearful, yet fascinating, mystery. We may still call such an experience 'religious' if we so wish. It is indeed humbling and spell-binding. But the cause and object of the experience are not 'religious' in the more usually accepted sense of the word. There is no God, there is only Sea. Nature-'worship' is no true worship of God. Indeed, the believer will be the first to affirm that it is idolatry.

Again, if in our discussion of 'religious' experiences we are inclined to characterise them by the transforming effects which they have on those who undergo them, on their power of conversion, then we must extend the class of such experiences so as to embrace the whole range of what Abraham

Maslow has called 'peak' experiences, many of which have not obviously anything directly to do with God at all.

> It has been discovered that this same kind of subjective experimental response (which has been thought to be triggered only in religious or mystical contexts, and which has, therefore, been considered to be only religious or mystical) is also triggered by many other stimuli or situations, e.g. experiences of the aesthetic, of the creative, of love, of sex, of insight, etc. If we insist on calling the peak-experience a religious experience, then we must say that religious experiences can be produced by sexual love, or by philosophical insight, or by athletic success, or by watching a dance performance, or by bearing a child.[7]

Of course it might still be argued that, however produced, they are in fact experiences of God. However, they are rarely apprehended as such by those who have them. To say the very least, they are inherently ambiguous.

The half-believer has a further, more personal, problem with religious experience. He doubts whether he himself has ever had a sense of the presence of God. Numinous experiences, which may dispose towards theistic belief, have played little if any part in his autobiography. He knows what it is from time to time to be moved to wonder, but he can hardly say that reflection on the starry heavens above or on the moral law within (to take but two examples) fill his mind with that ever new and increasing admiration and awe which they occasioned in Immanuel Kant. In short, he is disposed to admit that

> the methods of religion do not seem to be in the same way [as the methods of science] a disciplined and inter-

connected extension of everyday methods of reliable perception'.[8]

If religious perception cannot afford the same firm basis for religious belief as sense perception affords for scientific belief, is there a basis to be found in non-religious perception and argument, in natural theology or in revelation? Concerning the latter, it must be said that some reason is needed for believing that God exists before any experience or event can reasonably be entertained as a revelation of God. Concerning the former, the basic if often unconfessed premise of all natural theology is that the world *needs* to be explained. This is part of what is intended in speaking of its contingency. But does it need explaining? May it not itself be the ultimate, and, for us, necessary fact? And may not an assertion of the contingency of the world be a consequence of belief in God, precisely because it is held to depend upon his creative will, rather than a premise from which belief in God can be derived? In order for argument for God to get off the ground it seems that we need some kind of concomitant experience which at least will give it a motive force, even though it will not guarantee its cogency. At the very least there must be some movement of the mind which prompts it to question whether the observed world is to be taken as the ultimate 'given' or not.

We seem at this point to be moving inexorably back towards some appeal to experience; no longer, however, in any clearly isolated and self-authenticating form, but in close connection with our attempts to reflect, understand and explain. Such a move is indeed to be welcomed. For if belief in God is to be something more than a metaphysical theory concerning the higher administration of the universe, if it is to inform a religion which is not only a creed but also a way of life, a way of life for the individual inquirer, then the language and practice of that religion must be earthed in his lived experience. Those who say that they have no need of religion have at least some grasp of what religion is all about.

If religious belief is to be *understood*, it must be made clear to what sort of human experience it is to be related. If this cannot be done, it lapses into meaninglessness, or becomes a theological game, governed by its own internal rules, but inapplicable to the human situation. Religious beliefs require a context of experience in which they can be appropriated.

> Meanings arise, to be sure, in a community of discourse. But at the most fundamental level they represent not only the lateral sharing of recognized usage, but also the interaction of symbols to our felt experience, the symbol providing thematic and so communicable form to the stream of experience, and *both* are essential if there is to be meaning at all.[9]

There may be a sense in which it is perfectly proper to affirm that I must believe in order to understand, but there is a more obvious and more fundamental sense in which I must understand in order to believe. I cannot believe what I in no way understand, for I do not know what it is that I am invited to believe. And how am I to understand if what I am invited to believe makes no contact whatsoever with my own experience?

If experience is relevant to the understanding of religious belief, may it also be relevant to the *testing* of religious belief? At the heart of Christian faith is a gospel—a proclamation, a call and a promise. There is an offer of life and salvation. It is assumed that man is in some sense in bondage, that he needs to be delivered. It is declared that he can be made alive, that he can be saved. The gospel is meant to be put to the test. Is it correct in its analysis of the present human condition? Here an appeal to experience is possible, though not straightforward, for the blind may think that they see and the dead may think that they live. Is its promise of life and salvation trustworthy? Here too an appeal to experience is possible, although again it will not be straightforward, for much will depend on how the gospel promise is to be understood. If 'life' means life after death, then testing must await the hour of our death, unless it is believed that there can be communication between the living and the departed. But if 'life' is to be anticipated in the here and now, a pledge of the Parousia, then the gospel promise can in measure be tested here and now. Moreover, if the gospel is not to be accepted on bare authority, then the believer or would-be believer will treat the successful outcome of such preliminary and partial tests as an invitation to believe in the fullness of the as yet unfulfilled promise. If a father promises his son that he will be able to swim ten lengths of the baths, the son will begin to mistrust his father if he goes under every time that he enters the water. But if one day he discovers that he can already swim a width, then his father's promise that he will be able to swim ten lengths becomes so much the more credible.

Let us return to our half-believer. One thing that he clearly lacks is certainty. Of a faith which chooses with assurance and without misgivings he knows nothing. Nor is he able to distinguish sharply between sureness in religion and tentativeness in theology, between a basic self-authenticating intuition and its subsequent arguable interpretation. Nor can he draw a line of demarcation between intellectual difficulties and existential doubt.

Experience and interpretation interpenetrate and condition each other, they cannot be rudely prized apart.

What then may he hope for? What solution of his problems may he seek? Certainly not demonstrable proof or indisputable answer. They are simply not available. There remains only the venture of a human life, in fidelity to insight and understanding. Where no foolproof answers are forthcoming, and doubt is the anvil on which ultimate judgements and decisions must be forged, what he may hope for, the goal at which he must aim, is some integration of experience and understanding, of belief and action, in an intelligible form of life which offers him his personal identity and his world its enduring significance. What this identity and what this significance will be he has yet to discover. It could be courage in the face of an indifferent universe. It could be peace in the stilling of desire. It could be a number of things. Could it also be joy in the love and service of God?

2

THE QUESTION OF MAN

My soul thirsts for God, for the living God. When shall
I come and behold the face of God? My tears have been
my food day and night, while men say to me continually, 'Where is your God?'   (Ps. 42.2–3)

The question about God is also, though not exclusively, a
question about man. In his sensitive and searching book on
contemporary images of men, suggestively entitled *To Deny
our Nothingness*, Maurice Friedman has written:

Whatever may be the case with 'religion', the religious
man has always been aware of the central importance of
the image of man. This is because the religious life is not
in the first instance philosophy or gnosis—an attempt to
know *about* the world or God—but a way that man walks
with God, a flowing with the Tao, a discovery of 'the
action that is in inaction, the inaction that is in action'.
For the religious man, it is not enough to have a 'philosophy of life': one must live one's philosophy. Rabbi
Leib, son of Sara, went to the Maggid of Mezritch not to
hear him say Torah but to watch him lace and unlace his
felt boots. 'Not to say Torah but to be Torah'—this is the

existential demand that all religion ultimately places on man.[1]

If questions are to be answered, they must first be heard and understood. Even if God must somehow disclose himself in order to confront man as man's questioner, it remains true that, if the question is to be heard by men, it must find expression somewhere within the structures of human experience and understanding. A God inaccessible to human experience and understanding might still be 'God', the unknown and the unknowable, but he would be no God for man, the proper object of adoration and obedience. He would mean nothing to man. Where, then, is there room for his presence to be discerned, his voice to be heard? If the world which we inhabit has lost its enchantment and no longer rings with the echoes of divinity, is there perhaps a still small voice to be heard in the heart and mind of man himself? Does he as subject, if no longer as object, as agent, if no longer as event, have access to the court of heaven? If God is silent in the world outside, does he yet speak to the spirit of man within?

The loss of any sure and abiding sense of the presence of God in the world outside is linked with our scientific ways of understanding that world. Things are what they are, and events occur as they do, because there are discoverable patterns and regularities in all that happens. The world, when carefully observed and causally explained, reveals itself as a vast, orderly system of interlocking energies. The scientific description and explanation of this world do not need the hypothesis of God. Since he is not part of this world, he has no part in its description and explanation. Indeed, in this method of understanding the world it might more accurately be said that there is a need of a 'no-God' hypothesis.

For in this method of explaining what and how things are the introduction of a hypothetical God, who could cause anything to happen at any time and in any place, would hinder rather than further explanation. He would be a kind of pseudo-scientific joker. Capable of 'explaining' everything, he would in fact explain nothing.

If, then, our scientific understanding of what there is in the world, and how it functions, leaves no room for the question of God even to arise, shall we fare any better if we turn our attention from the world to man himself? Unfortunately, any hopes that we might have entertained seem to be doomed to an early disappointment. There is nothing to prevent the same kinds of method which we use in our understanding of the world from being used in our understanding of man. After all, man is just as much a part of the observed world as any other object. What once seemed to be inexplicable, unpredictable and fundamentally mysterious human behaviour is slowly but surely, through the development of the human sciences, being reduced to some sort of intelligible pattern. The sciences of genetics, bio-chemistry, human biology, psychology and sociology not only link man ever more closely to the rest of nature, but also move our understanding of man, it seems inexorably, in the direction of a thoroughly determined object whose origin, development and behaviour are to be pin-pointed within a single, causally explicable natural order of things (however complex this order may be, and however much of this order still remains to be explained). Thus, for example, in a letter to *The Times*[2] outlining the evidence offered by the British Psychological Society to the Butler committee concerning the law relating to mentally abnormal offenders, we read that:

psychology sees the entire range of human behaviour as determined by potentially explicable and predictable processes. Understanding these, for disposal and treatment, means that changes in behaviour can in principle be brought about; already a great deal has been done to apply such theoretical principles practically.

There hardly seems room for the hand of God here, where a man is to be reckoned as the sum of his naturally determined behaviour. Indeed, one is inclined to comment that not only are we faced with the abolition of God, but at the same time and in the same way we are confronted with the abolition of man.

The whole man is identified with the observable man, and human action is identified with determined and determinable human behaviour. It is no wonder that the writers are also found to say that 'the present state of psychological knowledge would seem to make nonsense of the current concepts of responsibility and guilt'.

At this point, however, we come face to face with a basic paradox of thought and action, a paradox which has often been noted – one might say that the whole philosophy of Immanuel Kant had one of its roots in this paradox—but which has never satisfactorily been resolved. There seems to be a forthright contradiction between the presuppositions underlying the knowledge of man acquired through the human sciences and the presuppositions underlying the uses to which that knowledge is to be put. In terms of the first, human behaviour is causally determined; deliberate choice (except as another name for some aspects of a 'decision-making process'), autonomous action and individual responsibility are either excluded or else transformed beyond recognition. They belong to a world of seeming, of illusion, not to the world of knowledge and reality. In terms of the second, however, when the observer becomes the agent, their reality is at least tacitly assumed. To what uses shall we put our knowledge? What sort of society do we propose to establish? What goals are we, armed with this knowledge, to pursue? Expelled through the door, the practical concepts of freedom and responsibility return through the window. Basic paradoxes, then, are not the preserve of the theologian wrestling with the relationship of divine and human agency. They appear already in the area of man's active relationship to the world. Indeed, as Langdon Gilkey pungently remarks:

> a myth which promises to man freedom *over* necessitating destiny on the basis of man's complete subservience *to* necessitating determination is surely *less* intelligible than are even the most sharply paradoxical theological accounts of the puzzles of human freedom and divine grace'.[3]

What we have exposed before us here is a seeming conflict between, on the one hand, a theory of knowledge and reality structured on the basis of a scientific method of investigation and understanding and, on the other hand, the lived experience of man in his active dealings with the world around him. We might conceivably reject our lived experience as illusory. But in so doing we should cut off the roots not only of our ordinarily conceived actions, but also of our science itself. For the pursuit of scientific knowledge is itself a form of action. Even observation is an activity which calls for responsible care and attentiveness, for discrimination and judgement, rather than an impersonal, passive recording of momentary events and occurrences. Consequently, if the conflict is to be resolved at all—or if it is to remain creative rather than destructive—we must be prepared to enlarge our understanding of experience, knowledge and reality so as to include that which comes to awareness through reflection on our total, lived experience as men engaged in responding to the world around us as well as in observing it, as agents as well as observers.

In any attempt to map out the pervasive structures of man's experience of his world, account must be taken of man as subject, just as account must also be taken of the world as object. Subjectivity, in this sense, has its inherent structures, just as much as has objectivity. The task of spelling out these structures has been undertaken by phenomenologists and existentialists, and I have neither the time nor the expertise to retrace the ground which they have laboriously sought to mark out. Let me content myself with drawing attention to one or two of the central features of the picture that has emerged.

First, man has the ability to distance himself from the immediacy of experience. He can go beyond what is immediately presented to him through his senses; he can objectify the world around him; he can envisage possibilities as well as actualities; he can project his understanding and purposes into the future; he can change his world. Thus, while he is part of the world he inhabits, he can also reflect on his world, understand it and, in a sense, rise above it.

Secondly, man also has the ability to distance himself from what is immediately presented to him as himself. If he can 'rise above' his world, he can also 'rise above' himself. He is self-transcending. Thus he can not only change his world, but in the very process of changing his world he can also change himself. He is not completely bound to his past, however much his present is determined by his past. He is also, in principle, open to the future. Subject to the laws of

nature he is also a law unto himself. What he has in himself
the power to become is as constituent a part of his humanity
as what he already is. His story is not complete until the last
chapter has been written. We do not know what a man
really is until we know what he will become. Thus the language of being must include the language of becoming. If
the world is a process, a becoming, so also is man a becoming. But whereas the becoming of the world is in large part
fixed and impersonal, the becoming of man calls for his own
participation in the direction of the process and in the determination of its outcome. Man is called to respond, and in
responding to accept responsibility.

That man should count himself as responsive and responsible in some such way as I have been suggesting seems to me
as much a part of his identity today as is his scientific understanding of the natural world. Humanism and naturalism
may in the end turn out to be incompatible bedfellows. It
may be impossible to combine both views into one. Nevertheless, the insights which give rise to these views must
somehow be retained. Neither side of the paradox can be let
go if man is to affirm both his dignity and his rationality.
But what needs to be noted here and now is that humanism,
as much as naturalism, may be hostile to any belief in God.
For it is precisely this sense of man's self-transcending responsibility which has fed, and for many continues to feed,
one stream of atheism, namely, moral atheism.

Man, it is argued, cannot achieve his full humanity—that
which he has it in himself to become and which the structure
of his humanity calls him to become—if the ultimate and
supreme disposer of men and nations, of history as well as of
nature, is God. Therefore, in the name of man's humanity,
faith in God must be disavowed. If man is to become what
he is, there *must* be no God. The fact that religion survives,

and that men here and there continue to believe in God, is a sign of their alienation from their true humanity and is to be explained in terms of psychological or social deviation. But such deviation may be diagnosed for what it is. It is contingent and reversible. It forms no part of man's essential humanity, that humanity waiting to be realised.

That psychological and sociological accounts of the origins and functions of religious belief cannot be rejected out of hand is undeniable. Since Freud and Marx we have come to know more about ourselves and consequently to be less sure of ourselves. Belief in God may serve a variety of purposes which it does not consciously profess. The believer is not immune from self-deception. He may be heard to confess the deceits of the heart of man. That religion has a pathology no-one in his right mind could deny. But is it, as the moral atheist asserts, nothing but a pathology? Does self-deception penetrate to the very core of belief, to its living heart, to belief in God? Is it deviation from the way to true humanity, and not the way itself?

An attempt to counter the charge that it is deviation might be made on the following lines.

First, it might be admitted that belief in God is, humanly speaking, a kind of projection. But this in itself is not particularly surprising. As we have seen, it is part of the essential structure of our humanity to distance ourselves from the immediacy of experience and to project patterns of meaning and interpretation on the world around us. Only by so doing can we hope to bring some order into the blooming, buzzing confusion of our immediate experience and understand the structures of whatever is—the processes, the things, the persons, the 'world' with which we have to do. Even in the pursuit of scientific knowledge imagination, model-making, theory-building have their essential part to play. Thus we need not at the outset be afraid of describing religion as a human enterprise, or the idea of God as a human construct. What else could they be?

Secondly, it would have to be argued that the religious projection, the search for and identification of that which is ultimate and unconditioned in being and value, and which grounds all finite and conditioned entities, giving them their existence and significance, is itself an essential and inescapable, not an accidental and arbitrary act of our humanity. That is, man could not be the man he undoubtedly is without his making an implicit, if not explicit, acknowledgement of God. Such an acknowledgement need not wait on verification through observation and experiment. Indeed to expect such verification would be radically to misunderstand the concept and being of God. It would be to transpose to the realm of empirical inquiry, where verification was appropriate, what properly belonged to the *a priori* conditions of all human inquiry and action, including the activity of verification itself. It would be to seek the one unconditioned among the many conditioned, to situate God in the world rather than the world 'in' God.

Let us look at two such attempts to proceed along these lines, to establish the reality of God as the unconditioned ground of all human thought and action, that without which man could not raise the question of God or even deny his existence. The first attempt derives from reflection on man as intelligent inquirer, the second from reflection on man as moral agent.

First, then, let us consider what Michael Novak has called 'the drive to question'.[4] Man is a creature who asks questions and seeks answers. The questions which he asks and the answers which he seeks are often circumscribed. They occur within a limited horizon which establishes the specific shape of his inquiry. This limited horizon is determined by his own interests and point of view, while itself determining the object of his inquiry. It sets the stage for his specific questions and answers. If the inquirer is to pass from mere opinion to well-grounded knowledge, he must submit himself to a certain discipline. In Bernard Lonergan's terminology he must be 'attentive, intelligent, reasonable, responsible'.[5] He must press his questions until he is satisfied that in his ensuing judgement everything relevant to the immediate inquiry has been taken into account. Then, and only then, may he properly claim to know.

However, even when this process has been completed, further questions may still arise, for the initial inquiry has been conducted within a *limited* horizon. What of this horizon itself? What of his initial point of view, and the field of objects which it opened to his inquiry? The drive to question, once given its rein, cannot arbitrarily be brought to a halt. It is in principle unrestricted. In so far as it is also a serious determination to understand, in intention it aims at nothing less than the ultimate and unconditioned. Only the ultimate and unconditioned can satisfy the unrestricted drive to question. Hence the determination to understand, present in the simplest act of seriously asking a question, is implicitly an affirmation that what *is* can in principle be understood, that being is ultimately intelligible. Now the intelligibility of ultimate being is part of what is affirmed in belief in God. Consequently the reality of God is the unconditioned ground of man's existence as a being who raises questions.

Whatever, then, may be the case concerning man's emotional need for an ultimate security—a need which may or may not exist, and, if it does exist, may or may not be satisfied—it can be argued that, as a persistent inquirer, one whose act of questioning cannot itself be questioned without some further act of questioning, he conducts all his search for knowledge within an implicitly affirmed context of unconditioned truth and being, urged on by an unrestricted drive to question and to understand. He intends total intelligibility. He affirms it in the very act of questioning. He cannot consistently deny it. It seems only a short step from here to argue that, because the intelligent inquirer comes to affirm that something is the case when that something has disclosed its intelligibility, and because the demand for intelligibility is unlimited, then being itself must be ultimately intelligible, and the only ultimately intelligible being conceivable is that which transcends the radically contingent and in which essence and existence are one.

It may seem only a short step, but in fact it is doubtful whether it is anything of the kind. Granted that man possesses, or is possessed by, an unrestricted drive to question; granted also that the act of questioning itself presupposes a faith in intelligibility, an affirmation, a demand that what is can in principle be rationally understood; it does not seem to follow necessarily that this demand will in fact be met. Questions may not always lead to further questions; they may simply cease. The unrestricted desire to understand may give way to an acknowledgement and acceptance of the fact that there is that which cannot be understood. Hope may ultimately be unfulfilled. As Ronald Hepburn comments in a review of Bernard Lonergan's work:

> We can admit that our desire to know is 'unrestricted', and that a confidence in our finding ever more intelligible structures, as the range of our enquiry is continuously extended, is heuristically of the greatest value. I doubt, however, whether the gap has been closed between the

expression of such a confidence and hope and the very strong claim that being is intelligible through and through.[6]

We find ourselves, then, left in a position in which we may acknowledge the existence of a deeply human desire, a far-reaching hope, for ultimate unity and intelligibility. We may even venture to say that intelligent inquiry, when pressed to the uttermost and refusing to rest content within limited and unquestioned horizons, points us beyond the finite and conditioned towards the *possibility* of the infinite and unconditioned. But we cannot yet say whether this transcendent space is empty and void, or filled with the fullness of God.

We turn now to the second attempt to establish the reality of God as the unconditioned ground of all human thought and action. In this attempt attention is concentrated on man as moral agent, the seeker after righteousness. Just as the first argument for the reality of God proceeded from the lived experience of man as intelligent inquirer, and sought to lay bare the transcendental conditions grounding all such inquiry, so the second argument is cast in a similar form. It seeks to lay bare the transcendental conditions grounding man's lived experience of moral action.

The starting-point is the fact that men recognise beyond the forces of changing inclinations and wishes the moral claim of that which is good in itself and the moral obligation to pursue it even at the expense of self-interest. The argument is that reflection on this experience reveals an implicit and inescapable affirmation that our moral decisions have a point, not simply here and now, but in the ultimate order of things. Thus to express a moral response is at the same time to express, as the valid ground of our response, a confidence in that which originally evokes and ultimately confirms our moral life—that is, a confidence in God. So Schubert Ogden, for example, has argued that, if we take our moral experience seriously, faith in God is necessary and inescapable. Religious belief in God is a re-presentation of a natural, if implicit, human faith. He writes:

> Always presupposed by even the most commonplace of moral decisions is the confidence that these decisions have an unconditional significance. No matter what the content of our choices may be, whether for this course of action or for that, we can make them at all only because of our invincible faith that they somehow make a difference which no turn of events in the future has the power to annul . . . The one thing for which none of us can rationally decide, whatever his particular choices, is the eventual nullity of any of his decisions. Even the suicide who intentionally takes his own life implicitly affirms the ultimate meaning of his tragic choice'.[7]

From here the step to affirming the reality of God is short.

> It lies in the nature of this basic confidence to affirm that the real whole of which we experience ourselves to be parts is such as to be worthy of, and thus itself to evoke, that very confidence. The word 'God', then, provides the designation for whatever it is about this experienced whole that calls forth and justifies our original and inescapable trust.[8]

Have we, however, now gone too far and too fast? There is indeed a sense in which we do attribute to our moral decisions an unconditional significance. They matter. In certain instances they matter supremely. Here I stand: I can do no other. Let justice be done, though the heavens fall. If they did not 'ultimately' matter, we should scarcely think of them as *moral* decisions. They matter now. They matter to me. Perhaps they also matter in the life of our shared humanity. But that they matter in some further sense of 'ultimacy' which seems to underlie Ogden's affirmed confidence—of this I am not sure. Furthermore, even if in making a moral decision I am indeed implicitly affirming an ultimate confidence, can I be certain that this confidence is not misplaced? Is my confidence more than a hope, or a cry to heaven? In what sense is my trust 'justified'? And the suicide? Is his act of self-destruction really to be construed as a strange expression of inescapable trust in the whole of which he himself is a part, as a moral protest and so, implicitly, a moral affirmation? Or is he a man without faith and hope, for whom death seems preferable to life simply because nothing any longer matters? Has he perhaps peered into the ultimate and unconditioned, and discovered there nothing but a void and an abyss?

Once again, this time by the path of our moral decisions in the realm of values, we find ourselves brought beyond the relative and conditional to the edge of the absolute and unconditional; but we are still unable to say whether this transcendent space is empty and void or filled with the promise of blessing, a threat of resignation and despair or a ground for confidence and hope.

Our reflections on human subjectivity have not established for us the reality of God. Ambiguity remains. Perhaps, however, we have done something to suggest the context in which the question and the possibility of God arise. It is that fundamental context of the unconditioned and the unconditional in which human knowledge of the world and action in the world take shape and persist. It is the region of the ultimate and the inescapable.

It is present, as it always has been in human life, as a base, ground, and limit of what we are, as a presupposition for ourselves, our thinking, our deciding, and our acting—all of which are, to be sure, relative. The ultimate or unconditioned element in experience is not so much the seen but the basis of seeing; not what is known as an object so much as the basis of knowing; not an object of value, but the ground of valuing; not the thing before us, but the source of things; not the particular meanings that generate our life in the world, but the ultimate context within which these meanings necessarily subsist.[9]

In so far as man is an intelligent inquirer, God is the reality anticipated by his unlimited desire to understand. In so far as man is a responsible agent, God is the perfection anticipated by his unlimited desire for the good. But the question is not silenced. What are the status and significance of such 'anticipation'? Is it a useless passion to be 'God' rather than man, or is it the voice of God himself calling man to be a son? Ambiguity remains.

In answer to the question put to him by his Catholic friends, whence does Marxism derive its negative capability except from a presence which lies 'behind the question', Roger Garaudy once replied:

Marxism asks the same questions as the Christian does, is influenced by the same exigency, lives under the same tension towards the future. The crucial factor is that Marxism does not consider itself entitled . . . . to transform its question into answer, its exigency into presence. 'O ever-active Spirit, how I feel your presence!' wrote Goethe. Marxism, by reason of its Faustian and Fichtean inspiration, does not succumb to the temptation to affirm, behind the activity, a being who is its source. My thirst does not prove the existence of the spring. For the Marxist, the infinite is absence and exigency, while for the Christian, it is promise and presence.[10]

An infinite emptiness driving man to seek in himself and for himself a human fullness? Or an infinite fullness confronting man with the fact that in himself and for himself he can never attain human fullness, but drawing him into the fullness of a creature in responsive love and obedience to a loving Creator, grounding man's freedom in the abundance of the divine charity and meeting man's intrinsic need with the riches of the divine grace? Is the contradiction only verbal, or does it give rise to fundamentally different and ultimately irreconcilable forms of human life? Simply to raise this question and to intend it seriously is to suggest that the answer is not as obvious as might at first sight appear. For the believer it may appear to be a straightforward choice *either* for God *or* for man. Certainly God is, in a sense, over against man, his creator and his judge. But he is also for, with and in man, his reconciler and his enabler. Furthermore, in his experience of what he affirms to be life in grace even the believer must confess that the light of God appears at times as darkness, and the presence of God at times as absence. Even if, then, God is truly acclaimed as light and presence, man's relationship to this God is such as to compel us to acknowledge and to take proper account of the experience of darkness and absence, an experience well known not only to 'sinners' but also to 'saints'.

Where, in this debate, does the half-believer stand? The question of God remains for him a burning question, a question which will not go away and leave him in peace. He grasps what the question is about. It bears upon his basic response to life and touches the springs of his confidence and hope. If there is no God, he will not yield to a nihilistic despair. He will husband his resources of courage and determination. Whatever the truth may be, he values knowledge and freedom, the search for truth and a responsible and responsive human life. But both his knowledge and his freedom are limited. His knowledge remains partial and his freedom ambiguous. Simple observation shows that even the most reasonable and responsible of men can at times act irrationally and irresponsibly. Sin is a concept which is no stranger to his vocabulary. If man, and man alone, is the sole source of hope, then hope itself becomes ambiguous.

Can he then believe that the unconditioned and unconditional is God, is presence and promise? Certainly he has heard 'a rumour of angels',[11] and seen what look like signals of the transcendent. But the world without and the world within also speak of a divine absence, threatening destruction and opening up an ultimate emptiness and void. In heart and mind he finds himself moving towards God; but when he sees the wind and the waves, he begins to go under. Is there a hand to reach out and raise him up?

3

INTERIM FAITH?

Whence then comes wisdom? And where is the place of understanding? It is hid from the eyes of all living, and concealed from the birds of the air. Abaddon and Death say, 'We have heard a rumour of it with our ears.'   (Job. 28.20-22)

Where is wisdom to be found? Nothing seems more certain to the half-believer than that God, if God there be, remains mysteriously hidden. He has no direct and unmistakable experience of him. He is unable once and for all to establish his existence beyond doubt by inference and argument, whether from the world without or from the world within. If God has indeed revealed himself in times past, the conditions of his self-revelation have subjected it to the same ambiguity as besets the whole range of human experience. Is it dream or is it reality? Nevertheless, despite his continuing doubts the half-believer acknowledges within himself a thirst for truth and righteousness, a search for a firm ground for belief and action. Even his own doubt he doubts. What is it that will not allow the thirst to be quenched or the search to be abandoned? Where is wisdom to be found?

With the questioning of traditional absolutes, with the

recognition of the fact that human perception, understanding and values embody the relativities of differing
points of view, that structures of meaning and significance
have varied from culture to culture and even from individual to individual, man may well feel that he walks on
shifting sands and that he lacks any firm foothold. What is
to prevent his being swallowed up? All his old landmarks
have been undermined. Where formerly he lived in the presence of God, now he feels his absence. Where formerly he
heard a divine word, now he hears nothing, or perhaps the
echo of his own voice. Where formerly belief and trust were
second nature, now doubt and despair fit all too easily his
frame of mind.

> When there is no longer any sense of grandeur in the
> 'shining from shook foil,' or of splendor in 'the ooze of
> oil/Crushed,' when there is no longer any lively sense of
> 'the dearest freshness deep down things,' then a great des-
> cent has begun—into that deprived condition that Martin
> Heidegger would nominate as 'godlessness.'[1]

The drive to question and the discovery of his own freedom
assume the aspect of a curse rather than a blessing. He is
conscious of a sense of overwhelming loss. He is no longer
secure. In his fear and rage he is tempted towards a rebel-
lious nihilism. It is not God who in his absolute omnipotence creates good and evil, sets nature its bounds and
orders the life of man. It is he himself who is the master of
his own life. The image of the omnipotent and jealous God
must be recast in the image of omnipotent and self-assertive
man. The religious lie of absolute dependence must be coun-
tered by the secular truth of absolute independence. He
must create his own good and evil. If he cannot create, then
let him destroy. An act of destruction, if freely willed, is as

authentically an act of human freedom as an act of creation. The nothingness at the centre can be extended to the circumference. If he cannot quite be God, he can at least be Lucifer. He can pull the world down around him in ruins.

If nihilism offers the only image of man that can survive the dissolution of the former absolutes, an image which demonically mirrors that which it seeks to displace, then it is hardly surprising that many should wish to retrace the steps of man's historical pilgrimage and to re-establish the old authorities or to invent new ones in their place. But there can be no return to an age of innocence. Man cannot repress the knowledge of himself and his world to which he has attained. There is no going back. He must venture forward into the wilderness in search of a promised land.

Nihilism, however, is not the only alternative option open to one who has experienced the dissolution of his traditional absolutes. No doubt the experience itself strikes home as a real threat to human security and significance. No doubt some, perhaps many, when they find themselves and their accustomed world so threatened, are tempted by their fears towards some nihilistic act of self-assertion, and they may even find a strange satisfaction in destruction for destruction's sake. The symptoms may be obscured in individuals and in society. Nevertheless, this destructive impulse resembles a tantrum rather than an action, a display of would-be childish omnipotence rather than a mature and responsible human choice. For faced with the demand to make his own value judgements, to construct his own human world, to shoulder the responsibility for his own future, man is left with the choice whether to build up or to tear down. If he cannot have God, he need not be Lucifer. He may still be man, accepting both the limitations and the potentialities of his own humanity.

Language about the threat of nothingness or the abyss of an ultimate void may have its use in shaking men out of their complacencies or in exposing their idolatries, but it can be overdone. To say that it can be overdone is not to deny that some may in fact experience an utter pointlessness in their lives and lose all sense of personal identity and worth. Nor is it to deny that human life is beset with ills and accidents, failures and disasters, that the individual will sooner or later die and the whole human race will one day almost certainly vanish off the face of the earth. Nor, again, is it to deny the truly tragic dimension of man's life, when the discovery of a truth or the achievement of a good carries in its train disintegration rather than healing. But it is to deny that, when the traditional concepts of absolute and ultimate truth and goodness are put in question, nothing of value remains.

What remains is a fundamental distinction between knowledge and ignorance, rationality and irrationality, truthfulness and deception, a distinction the validity of which it is impossible seriously to deny, since it is presupposed by any life which could conceivably be called 'human'. There is still a better and a worse. Perfection may perhaps be an illusion, and the desire for perfection a sickness of the soul. Utopia may be a harmless or a cruel dream. But men can become better or worse men, and some societies are better to live in than others. Even if we grant that in the long run we shall all be dead, there is still the short run. Even if we are all journeying towards the world's end, our several journeys may lead us by a variety of different routes. To say that life is through and through absurd, because there are no longer any obvious and universally recognisable absolutes, no transcendent realm of pure truth, beauty and goodness, and that consequently nothing really matters, is to ignore the fact that by their very actions men declare that some things do matter to them. If nothing really mattered, men might continue to behave mechanically. But no-one would *do* this rather than that because he *wanted* to do this rather than that. In fact, for everyone many and various things matter.

The problem is not one of *making* things matter. The problem is rather one of determining our priorities, of reflecting on the things which already matter to ourselves and to others, of discovering new things which also matter, and of deciding how all these are to be ordered coherently, if at all possible, in relation to one another. In asking and answering the question what really matters we establish an order of values and adopt a way of life. We express this way of life, individually and communally, in the actions which we perform and in the structures and institutions which we shape. In this way we construct the human world which together we inhabit, and in so doing contribute to the making of ourselves and of our fellow-men. In this sense it is correct to say that, while men are made by history, history is also made by men. Man is creative, and his creativity extends to his own humanity. Nevertheless, his creativity occurs within a context of acceptance and response. He creates as he discovers. Receptivity and creativity are interwoven. It is at least misleading, therefore, if not downright false, to say without careful qualification that, once he has recognised that he is free to make his own decisions about the future, he must create his own values. For he cannot simply *decide* that something shall matter to him if it does not in virtue of its own character already matter to him. He might indeed *pretend* that something mattered, but that would be the beginning of deception and falsehood. He might, without deception, *act as if* something mattered to him in the hope that it would come to matter to him. This is often the way by which we come to recognise new values. In neither case, however, is there any basis to be found for affirming that man arbitrarily creates his own values.

Men first acquire their values through nature and nurture. These are rooted in their biological, psychological and social needs and satisfactions. They are in this sense 'given'. But they are not simply and unalterably 'given'. For men may question the values which they have received and the practices in which they are embodied. They are not totally bound to the past, whether their own or that of the culture in which they have grown up. The same drive to question which has dislodged the traditional absolutes from nature and from history has also revealed to man that he is not a helpless prisoner of the past, destined to play out his future in the roles which he has inherited from his past. What he may yet become is as definitive of his humanity as what he has already been. If the past is closed, the future remains open, *his* future in a sense significantly different from that in which the past is his past. As Garaudy has expressed it:

> Transcendence is man's chief attribute inasmuch as he alone, unlike animals confined within the cycle of repetitive behaviour, is a being who can take stock of his purposes beforehand and by his efforts achieve something new. This transcendence is an everyday experience, present in every creative act: whether in the artist's creation, or in the research of the scientist or the technologist, or in love, sacrifice, or revolution; in everything, that is to say, where we break out of the circle of positivist knowledge and rise above purely utilitarian actions designed to satisfy needs that belong to the past.[2]

Man is a self-transcending animal, open to the future. But

if the future is on this account and to this extent indeterminate, how is man to determine it? It is at this point that his moral dilemma arises. Where there is no predetermined goal, how shall he know in which direction to proceed? Not everything that is old is bad, and not everything that is new is good. Bare self-transcendence is ambiguous. It opens possibilities both for creation and for destruction. Where is wisdom to be found?

First, there must be a realistic acknowledgement not only of human potentialities but also of human limitations. Man's life is embedded in the natural world, and nature itself sets bounds to what man can hope to achieve. Nature may indeed be plastic, but it is not infinitely plastic. Man must work with the grain of things, not against it. Furthermore, he himself is not pure spirit with the powers of absolute freedom. He is embodied spirit, or inspirited body. His experience, understanding and values, though open to an unbounded horizon, themselves remain bounded and finite. He must never forget that he is man and not God.

> Once this element of self-criticism in all human thinking is ignored, once we claim proprietary rights over reality so as to be able to declare what it is, once we claim to be the interpreter, the spokesman and even the agent of the absolute, we are on the direct road to the Inquisition or to Stalinism.[3]

Such self-criticism requires a high degree of truthfulness and courage—truthfulness to expose the insidious workings of our fears and conceits, courage to accept the discipline demanded by the truth thus exposed.

Second, the faculty to criticise must be supported and complemented by the faculty to construct and to create. In fact the critical and the constructive should be seen as obverse and reverse sides of one and the same coin. They are properly moments in a single responsive activity. Responsible criticism is not criticism for criticism's sake. It points beyond what is, to what may yet become. It exposes the inadequacies of present beliefs and practices in the hope that they may be transformed and integrated into a fuller understanding and a richer life. It seeks a deeper knowledge and a better way. Experience and reflection may render a belief no longer tenable or a practice no longer tolerable. It is always possible for a man to deny the experience, to regret the knowledge and to continue in the same old way. But he who has set out along the path of righteousness and truth may not look back, however inviting the comforts of an Egyptian slavery may appear in comparison with the hardships of a desert pilgrimage. He must press on towards a deeper understanding and a more adequate pattern of values which will do justice to the new experience and knowledge as well as the old. No doubt this new knowledge and these new values will in time come to reveal their own inadequacies. Then the process of criticism and construction must be carried on afresh. It does not come to a sudden end. New horizons are always opening up. There are oases and resting-places, but there is only a rumour of a promised land.

Third, both as thinker and as doer man needs the community of his fellow-men. Even the pursuit of scientific knowledge generates its own ethic as a presupposition of scientific inquiry. As Bronowski has put it:

> Science cannot survive without justice and honor and respect between man and man . . . [it] must prize the search above the discovery and the thinking (and with it the thinker) above the thought. In the society of scientists each man, by the process of exploring for the truth, has

earned a dignity more profound than his doctrine.[4]

If the dignity of the individual man and the values and imperatives which sustain it are presupposed by the activity of man the scientific inquirer, they are equally presupposed by man the doer and maker of history. Self-knowledge is a prerequisite of responsible and responsive action. If each man is to discover his own identity and his individual dignity, he will do so only through his relationships to others who acknowledge and ascribe to him that dignity. In the immediate family circle he learns to love, himself and others, because he is first loved. In the larger circles of his relationships he comes to regard and be regarded because he participates in a community in which such regard is constitutive of that community. Such mutual regard in one sense sets limits to the way in which a man may treat other men. To treat another as if he were only an object to be manipulated for one's own purposes is a failure in human regard. It reduces the agent as well as the patient to something less than a person. In another sense mutual regard extends the limits set by mutual affection and interest. It involves the category of the neighbour. It opens up the possibilities of an extended and deepened humanity. It embraces the present *and* the future.

Fourth, a man's recognition of his fellow-men as persons like himself, as sharing a common humanity, prompts him to move outward from his own experience and point of view to share in others' experience, to see things from their point of view, to feel their hopes and fears as his own hopes and fears, to enter into and to understand their beliefs and values. Thus his own narrow individuality is transcended and his own experience and understanding enriched. He loses himself in the life of others. He moves from the particular towards the universal—not the universal in the sense of some abstract humanity, but in the sense of a rich and variegated life which throbs through a whole family of related and yet distinct particulars. In so losing himself, however, he also finds himself afresh. There is a double movement, in which the individual proceeds from himself and returns to himself again. There is a coming and a going within the human family. In going out from himself he listens to the other, feels and experiences with the other, identifies himself with the other. In coming back into himself he re-establishes his own point of view and his own individuality. But in his returning he brings something of the other with him. The insights with which he began the dialogue are no longer precisely the same. Something new has in the process been added to himself, something which now in turn can be offered to others.[5]

What I have been trying to suggest is that man does not lack all sense of direction when he moves into the as yet undetermined future. There are signposts. There is a compass, even if there is no itinerary. The future need not be a vain and continuing repetition of the past. There is the possibility of creative self-transcendence. Man must be willing to turn outwards from himself towards his neighbour, so that both he and his neighbour together can discover a new humanity. He must be willing to open himself to the call of a new future, a ready listener to those who see visions and dream dreams, be they poets or prophets or politicians. He must possess and be possessed by what has been called 'a passion for the possible'. He must cherish integrity and hope.

To place such emphasis on the possibility of creative self-transcendence, to speak in the same breath of seeing visions and dreaming dreams, to urge the fundamental importance of integrity and hope, at once suggests that we have escaped from sober reality into a world of our own make-believe while covering our flight with a cloak of pious but powerless moral exhortation. The charge is serious and must be seriously faced. Hope can indeed be a form of self-delusion. It must secure its own ground. Whether self-transcendence provides that firm ground for hope, or whether it is provided only by the absolute transcendence of God, is one aspect of the debate between belief and unbelief. It is important, however, that the debate should not be conducted in the wrong terms. In stressing the power of creative self-transcendence and man's openness to the future the humanist does not for one moment wish to deny that man must take full cognizance of the past and the present. The future may be open, but it is not totally open. The past is a determining factor in shaping the future. Often, indeed, it is the determining factor. Consequently, if man is to discover a way forward in his gropings, he must be as sensitive to the actualities of the present as to the possibilities of the future. He must listen as intently to those who analyse the present in the light of the past as to those who appraise it in the light of the future. He must reckon with the workings of nature and the forces of history. He must extend his scientific knowledge to its limits. If he dares to hope for creative advance, he must at least seek to understand the conditions which render such advance possible. If he has his head above the clouds, he must keep his feet firmly on the ground. But men are more than objects. They are also subjects. If they are to exercise their freedom responsibly as subjects, they must continually hold before themselves the ends to which they aspire and for which they are prepared to work, ready to receive the new vision and the fresh insight, from whatever sources they may spring. Where there is no vision, there the people perish. Moral exhortation may or may not have a validity of its own, granted the right time and the right place. What is wrong with it is surely not its call to responsibility, but rather its temptation to forget that what is primarily needed is a new vision, and a new commitment in response to that vision, rather than a redoubled effort in pursuit of the old vision. It is precisely the old vision which prevents creative advance and renders the future still-born. Thus vision and commitment, call and obedience, belong together. True prophecy is both seeing and summons.

At this point in the discussion the 'true' believer may interject. 'You have made out a fair case', he may say, 'for openness towards the future and towards the neighbour, for integrity and hope, even though you claim to have derived these imperatives from your much-vaunted human self-transcendence, from the drive to question and to understand, and from what you term the call of the future, rather than from the revealed will of God. But it is precisely here that your humanism, if you will pardon the word, comes to grief. For man is unable in his own strength to walk the path that you have marked out for him. At the root of his troubles there is a mortal sickness, namely, his proud and wilful self-assertion, his disobedience towards God. His self-centredness, his heart and mind turned in upon himself, render null and void all his attempts to open himself to the true source of his life. Even self-abnegation becomes an inverted form of self-assertion. He is in fact a prisoner of his own self. Hence he is powerless to follow the way of life which you have depicted, because it is his very self-centredness which sours and sullies even his noblest efforts. He can be saved only from beyond himself, only by God. For only God can forgive, heal and restore him at the centre of his being.'

If this is indeed an accurate description of the human

predicament, then man may well despair of his humanity and in his despair cry out to God for salvation. There can be no other exodus. There must be death to the old man and a re-creation of the new. But is the description accurate? Is it to be taken just as it stands, sharply drawn in an opposing black and white? Does the alleged self-imprisonment of unbelieving man show itself in experience and life as utterly destructive as this picture suggests? Correspondingly, does the alleged re-creation of believing man show itself in experience and life in such obvious manner that the new can be clearly contrasted with the old, the redeemed with the unredeemed? If experience is to be accepted in any way as a proper criterion, if the tree is to be judged by its fruits, then surely the picture must be re-drawn in subtler and more converging shades rather than in its original stark black and white. If the fruits of belief are perhaps not as unambiguously good as the believer might have us think, the fruits of unbelief are perhaps not as unambiguously rotten.

No-one wishes to affirm that man is naturally a saint and that it is only ignorance that prevents his innate goodness from shining forth in a dark world. Self-centredness is an undeniable fact. Man is limited in his sympathies as well as in his rationality. He can be abysmally indifferent to the needs of others. History as well as individual experience reveals that this is so. Nevertheless, it does not seem to be the case that all men are always and inevitably self-centred, that in them there is no good thing at all. Many examples could be adduced to show that somehow, perhaps quite often, they give themselves whole-heartedly to and for others in acts of sacrificial love. The persistent cynic may insist that there are always hidden, selfish motives underlying such apparently unselfish actions, but there is no good reason to believe that the cynic must be right. Only dogma can convert a 'sometimes' into an 'always'.

Selfishness and unselfishness are both to be found in the human heart. Nor does it seem to square with experience to say that only God can forgive man for his self-centredness. Surely men themselves can learn to forgive each other and so to repair the damage which self-centredness has done to human relationships of love and regard. There is such a reality as natural grace.

What, however, of the charge that man has disobeyed God, and that only the supernatural grace of God can forgive and restore this fundamental relationship, the breaking of which distorts and damages all other and lesser relationships? It is, of course, difficult, if not impossible, to make sense of such an assertion except from within the circle of belief. For where or what is this God whom, it is alleged, man has disobeyed? The story of Adam's fall is not to be taken literally. Even if we take it symbolically as the story of every man, we do not find in each individual history any act of deliberate disobedience towards God. God is not known or recognised as God. Perhaps, however, God speaks and a voice is heard, a voice whose authority is acknowledged, even though it is not recognised as the voice of God. Suppose, for example, that a man recognises a call, coming to him through the circumstances of his own life and his own growing self-consciousness, to respond with heart and soul and mind to the opportunities and challenge of his world at those points where openness, love and creativity beckon; and suppose, as all too often seems to be the case, he refuses the responsibility, responding not at all, or inadequately, or too late. Might such be a kind of original sin which no human forgiveness can absolve?

I am inclined to take this suggestion seriously, and to say that here lies the measure of man's ultimate irresponsibility, exposing a guilt which is no mere neurotic disease. Such guilt cannot be shrugged off with a casual act of repentance and a determination to do better the next time round. Nor can it be counted as a circumstantial fact about the human condition, something that simply happens to men, as death may be said to happen to them. For it is his own determination, his own response or failure to respond, which is here at issue. It is not something that merely happens to him, however much he is tempted to shift the responsibility off his own shoulders and to throw the blame on external forces of evil. 'The woman whom thou gavest to be with me, she gave me fruit of the tree, and I ate.' . . . 'The serpent beguiled me, and I ate.' To deny responsibility at this point is to opt for something less than his birthright as a person. On the other hand, to accept responsibility is to be his own judge and in his own eyes to stand condemned. How, then, can he both accept and condemn himself as the person that he is at one and the same time? It is not a question of courage, a courage, for example, by which he might accept the fact of his own death as part of the human condition. He cannot accept his own guilt in the way in which he might accept his own death. It is a question of forgiveness. And if he is in no position to forgive himself, how can forgiveness be forthcoming? The judgement stands. Only a faith which can accept that he is accepted can avail him. But can such faith be other than make-believe if there is no saving God?

Reflections such as these deserve, as I have suggested, serious consideration. Nevertheless, it must at the same time be thankfully admitted that, in forgiving one another, in caring for one another regardless of deserts, men do from time to time enable each other to accept themselves and to draw once again from the well of life. Perhaps they are ministers of a grace which is more abundant than their own.

This brings me to my final point. It must never be forgotten that the creative vision of what is not yet but which may come to be, a vision which is vouchsafed to a few as and when the spirit stirs, and which can be communicated by them to others less favourably blessed, inspiring a new and more radical commitment, is not something which a man can manufacture and control by his own act of will. It comes to him as a gift, evokes response and issues in action. It both humbles and exalts. Thus the integral act of creative self-transcendence is his and yet is not his. His was the response, but whence came the gift? Was it of man, or was it of God? If we say 'of man', then it was from a level of his being which was deeper than his conscious self and beyond his rational control. If we say 'of God', are we doing more than use a hallowed symbol to express our sense of wonder at the resources of receptivity? What is, however, certain is that in either case man has no cause for overweening pride. Life comes to him from beyond his immediate self.

The way of transcendence, of openness to experience, the neighbour and the future, has about it something of the character ascribed to the experience of the numinous. It is both inviting and frightening, *fascinans et tremendum*. The emptiness left behind by the disappearance of the traditional absolutes carries with it a sense of loss, possibly of anxiety. At the same time it promises liberation from idols and engenders hope for humanity. Thus the emptiness is itself ambiguous and the hope uncertain. What awaits man as he ventures forth to receive his inheritance, not knowing where he is to go?

4

GROUNDS FOR HOPE

You must work out your own salvation in fear and trembling; for it is God who works in you, inspiring both the will and the deed, for his own chosen purpose.   (Phil. 2.12–13; *NEB*)

The question which the half-believer finds himself asking is not 'Man *or* God?', as if a decision for God were at the same time a decision against man, but rather 'What manner of humanism?' In shaping the question thus he is asking after the source, centre and goal of human existence. He is approaching the question of God indirectly through the question of man. Such an approach ought not to seem strange to a faith which proclaims that God became Man and looks to its fount and origin in one whose name was Emmanuel, God with us.

There have been, however, and still are, movements in Christian thought which seek to establish the reality of God on the basis of the unreality of man. Their premise is what Anthony Dyson has called 'the thesis of the negativity of all human existence before God'.[1] According to this thesis there is nothing in the ambiguities of human experience, in nature, history or the human soul, which can so much as point towards a knowledge of God. Only God himself can penetrate the human darkness, and that only through a unique and discontinuous act of revelation, to be apprehended by an equally unique and discontinuous act of faith. Natural religion is nothing but idolatry, natural morality nothing but filthy rags, a vain attempt by man to cover his sin and to justify his godlessness. Only when he has been thoroughly convicted of his nothingness, and driven to the ultimate limits of despair, only then will he be ready to abandon himself without further question or struggle to the totally other God and accept his offer of salvation.

Some, maybe, will find here a picture of true religion and of authentic faith. Indeed, it possesses a strange grandeur of its own. God is infinitely exalted as God; he is no mere adjunct of man. Faith is utter obedience to God; it is not for man to strike up some bargain. God is all, man is nothing. Only the self-noughting of man can make room for God. Is not this the essence of Christian belief and devotion?

Appealing though this picture may appear, not least in its determination to let God be very God, other than and independent of man, Judge as well as Saviour, nevertheless it is purchased at a price—and that a price which many will be unwilling to pay. For it puts the decision of faith beyond all reason and argument. It makes it impossible to discriminate between rival claims to revelation. It disallows any authority to man's own insights into truth and goodness, gained through history and culture and sifted through critical reflection.

Yet it is precisely by an appeal to such insights that Christians down the ages have sought to develop their understanding of the will and purpose of God. A revelation which does not in any way make sense of human experience and understanding, even as it challenges and transforms it, is scarcely a revelation at all. It does not connect. It cannot be appropriated and integrated into the totality of human life. It may overwhelm, but it can hardly raise up. It is intrusive and alien. A gulf is set up between God and man which not even God himself can bridge. There is no need to disown the authentic desire to acknowledge the ultimacy and freedom of the divine initiative in creation and redemption and so to ascribe to God the glory due to his being—'not to us, O Lord, not to us, but to thy name give glory'[2]—but, as has been aptly remarked, it is an odd way of exalting the Creator to denigrate his creature. Creation and redemption must not in this violent manner be prized apart. Continuity must not be denied in the process of recognising discontinuity. Fallen man and redeemed man are both significantly man. They have certain insights and values in common. Hence for theological as well as for ethical and epistemological reasons it is necessary to reject the thesis of the negativity of all human existence before God.

We turn, therefore, from the mistaken and misleading question, 'Man *or* God?', and ask the different, though possibly still misleading, question, 'What manner of humanism?'

To phrase the question thus is not to decide in advance in favour of unbelief rather than of belief. It is to seek to establish a common ground from which discussion may begin. There are varieties of humanism, just as there are varieties of Christianity. Humanism may find articulation and expression in a number of related but distinctive ideologies and programmes, just as Christianity may find articulation and expression in a number of related but distinctive theologies and ways of life. It is possible, however, to discern within the humanistic framework an underlying conception of the human condition and the human task, together with an associated set of human values, which I suggest, can be accepted by believer and unbeliever alike. As we have already seen, man is a questioning and self-transcending animal. As such he is called to respond in openness to the world, to his neighbour and to the future. Such response demands integrity, compassion and courage, a strong conviction of the dignity of the individual and an equally strong conviction of each individual's membership within the community of men. It is orientated towards the possibility of the new and the better. It presses beyond the limits of a morality based on reciprocity and justice, the necessary presupposition of any kind of social and co-operative activity, towards a morality which is creative and transforming and which calls for sacrifice and love, an 'open' rather than a 'closed' morality.

If such a conception of the human condition and the human task is to be accepted by believer and unbeliever alike, each must be willing to move out of certain entrenched positions and go some way towards meeting the other. As we have already seen, the believer must be asked to abandon the thesis of the negativity of all human existence before God. Man, even unbelieving man, is not bereft of valid insights into the shape and form of human flourishing, nor is he utterly impotent in the ways of truth and righteousness. Self-interest is not the only motive which he acknowledges for his actions, for 'self' is constantly being broken, refashioned and redefined by the persuasive invitation of that which transcends his own established interests. Natural grace may be rare, but it is nonetheless real despite its rarity.

On the opposing front the unbeliever must be asked to abandon, at least provisionally, his definition of humanism in terms of the non-existence of God. To ask the unbeliever to make this move may appear to him to be asking him to abandon the very core and centre of his position. However, the negation of God cannot of itself provide the substance and content of his humanism. It may have an important initial role in countering a belief in God which carries with it a radical negation of man; but once the believer has abandoned the thesis of the negativity of all human existence before God, this initial role is no longer necessary. The question of God can then be raised, not at the outset and before discussion has begun, but in the context of a shared exploration of man and his world on the basis of a common approach, an agreed understanding of the human condition and task.

Two points concerning this agreed understanding should be kept in mind. First, it is not a straightforward empirical description of what men always and inevitably are. If we affirm the dignity of man, and highlight such characteristics as his drive to question and to understand, his ability to transcend himself and his openness to the future, his moral insights into good and evil and his commitment to truth and righteousness, we are ourselves adopting a particular point of view and expressing a particular commitment. Other points of view and commitments are possible. In adopting ours we have in mind not so much what men actually are, although this of course cannot be ignored, for it forms part of our total understanding of men, but more especially what they have it in them to become, and what, if they are sensitive to the as yet unrealised, they are in some sense 'called' to become.

Second, this understanding of man is formative rather than concrete. He may indeed be called to respond creatively to the world, to his neighbour and to the future, but this will determine the *how* rather than the *what* of his response. The *what* has still to be determined. The direction has been indicated, but the path has to be cleared. Man finds himself existing in an already given world. This world can be changed but it cannot be ignored. It too contributes to man's future. Man's critical consciousness, his self-transcendence, is, writes Rubem Alves,

> on the one hand, determined by its apprehension of the inhuman and therefore contradictory character of society, and on the other, by the discovery of both the unfinished character of the world and the open horizons that invite man's creativity and experimentation. Like a lover, however, it does not allow its passion to remain subjective. It wants to fertilise the earth, to bear a child, to create a new tomorrow in which its negation and hope will become historical.[3]

In creating the new tomorrow man must have some understanding of the world which he is to shape, of its actualities and potentialities, as well as of his own actualities and potentialities. He does not act in a vacuum, nor is he pure spirit. It follows, therefore, that what we have called the underlying humanistic conception of man is bound to take on various specific shapes, and to assume various specific forms, according to the ways in which man and his world are perceived and intended.

Christian and secular 'humanism' may both be properly called forms of humanism in so far as both move outward from human experience, understanding and action to reflect on the nature of the world in which man lives, and neither begins with a dogmatic and *a priori* assertion either of God's existence or of his non-existence. However, whereas the Christian humanist goes on to affirm that nature, man and history are open to that which always and actually transcends them, to the reality of God, the secular humanist construes transcendence in terms of human potentiality, of the non-existent and the not-yet, and denies the reality of God. For the secular humanist, as J. P. van Praag rightly asserts, 'the world is complete'. And he adds, to make his point clear, 'completeness is not perfection, but means that the world is not thought of as dependent on a creator, nor is there an empty place left vacant by an absent creator'.[4] In the order of knowing both Christian and secular humanist begin with man and his world. In the order of being the Christian humanist affirms the prior reality of God, while the secular humanist ends where he begins. Secular humanism 'does not merely place man in a central position, but accepts him as the only possible foundation of human living'.[5] Thus in the working out of belief and practice, of attitude and expectation, the paths diverge. It is the nature of this divergence that I wish to explore. How wide is it?

Let us begin by considering some of the criticisms which are sometimes levelled by the Christian against his unbelieving brother.

First, it is sometimes asserted that the secular humanist has merely substituted Man for God, that the characteristics of freedom, creativity and self-determination, perhaps even of omnipotence, formerly ascribed to God, have now been abrogated by man to himself. 'Glory to man in the highest.' But this is not the case. Or at least it need not be the case. Secular humanism is not essentially a kind of titanism. It does not attempt to fill 'an empty place left vacant by an absent creator'. Childish fantasies of omnipotence may tempt both believer and unbeliever. They are the prerogative of neither.

Second, it is sometimes asserted that the secular humanist, despite his avowal that man is man and not a would-be God, fails to recognise, or at least to do justice to, the corruption in man and his fatal partiality for evil as well as for good. 'Secular humanism', writes V. A. Demant, 'evades the demonic possibility in our human existence. . . . There is potential demonism in human power, in knowledge, in technics, in sex, liable to take possession of the best in human beings.'[6] Is such a charge justified?

No doubt some secular humanists have been unrealistically optimistic in their assessment of man's future, led astray by the illusion of automatic and inevitable progress, whether through the evolutionary processes of nature or the dialectical processes of history. Others, again, may have seen in the triumphs of technology the promise of solving all human problems, given time, knowledge, money and power, and have failed to foresee that the structures and institutions devised by technological expertise to make men free may assume a dynamic and momentum of their own and enslave their makers. However, a blind optimism concerning man is not an essential feature of secular humanism. Indeed, to judge by contemporary literature—and the writer contributes to the humanist's self-understanding as well as the technologist—pessimism is as likely to be the prevailing mood as is optimism. Threat and despair are the notes which ring from its pages more clearly than hope and promise. If, then, Christian humanism has something to offer its secular counterpart, it might perhaps be some firmer ground beyond the shifting sands of optimism and pessimism, a more enduring and resourceful hope rather than a summons to confession of sin, a gospel rather than a law, although the two cannot be completely dissociated if truth and mercy are to meet together.

What, then, are the resources of courage and hope for secularist and Christian respectively? Are we to say that the secularist puts his faith in man's 'inextinguishable endeavour', while the Christian puts his in God's indefectible love; that the secular humanist hopes, because he can act, while the Christian humanist acts, because he can hope? Something like this, I believe, may and must be said. But it is important that it should not be said too quickly or too easily. For the secular humanist, too, has his own resources for the cleansing and renewal of human endeavour. There are, for example, the resources of inter-personal relationship. Men may correct, provoke, support, encourage and renew one another. That is, they may minister grace to each other. Or, again, there are the resources of the imagination, in nature and in art, which can purify thought and desire and turn men outwards from their own selfish and narrow interests. Creative action may derive from creative vision. Or, yet again, there is a kind of prayer, at least of meditation and contemplation. 'Whatever one thinks of its theological context', Iris Murdoch has written, 'it does seem that prayer can actually induce a better quality of consciousness and provide an energy for good action which would not otherwise be available.'[7]

Nevertheless, when all this, and more, has been said about the resources for man's renewal available to unbeliever and believer alike, the Christian will wish to go on to say that his deepest resource of courage and hope, if indeed it is to be called a resource, is not something which immediately bends back on his own consciousness and so becomes *his* resource, but is rather the recognition of a new and living centre of himself and his human world, with whom responsibility for the future, as for the past and present, ultimately rests, a responsibility in the exercise of which he himself can

61

ultimately trust. Thus at the centre of his own activity he rests in God, and it is this 'resting in God' which, far from cutting the roots of his own endeavour, is in fact the deepest resource of his hope and action. For now it is God who frees him from the alternating forces of optimism and pessimism which arise from within himself, reflecting his own achievements and failures, and so enables him to move forwards with hope along the path which opens in front of him. The affirmation of God offers man the possibility of *being free from himself*.

> This sense of freedom, of absolution [writes Henry McKeating,] is something which can rarely be got from any human relationship. I may feel great security in a human relationship, be it with my wife, my analyst, my probation officer or my priest. I may feel completely confident that in that relationship I am accepted as I am, and that I will not be rejected because of anything I have done or may do. I may experience a great feeling of relief or freedom on the confession of some particular sin that has burdened me or on the clearing up of some particular misunderstanding or in the making up of a quarrel. But what that relationship is less able to give me is the feeling of being free of myself, of being right with the world, and right with God.'[8]

The Christian wishes to affirm that at one and the same time God redeems the past and offers hope for the future, freedom from oneself and hence freedom to be and to become oneself. He believes that this is at its deepest level the outcome of perceiving and intending the world as God's world, the fruit of the prayer of faith, the forgiveness of sin and the promise of life. He could agree with Karl Britton when, in concluding his observations on religion and the meaning of life, he writes:

> A man who is himself a believer cannot suppose that in
> the eyes of God there is a fundamental difference between
> those who believe honestly and those who disbelieve hon-
> estly: between those who seek God's forgiveness and
> those who somehow learn to forgive themselves as well as
> to forgive others.[9]

Nevertheless, he would be emptying his faith of much of its
inherent content if he did not go on to affirm that there was
indeed a way of renewal and a resource of hope more radical
and far-reaching than that suggested by the 'somehow'.

There is yet a third criticism which is sometimes levelled
against the secular humanist; namely, that he has no 'answer' to the facts of evil and of death, and 'that only God . . .
meets the deepest longings of the human heart, which is
never fully satisfied by what the world has to offer'.[10] The
secular humanist will reply, as does von Praag, that:

> humanism does not pretend to give another answer to the
> questions put by traditional faiths. . . . The humanist is
> not a Christian stripped of his Christian expectations and
> attitudes; he has a different approach. Of course he does
> not deny evil, sorrow and death, but conceives them as
> the natural seamy side of his aspirations. As a painting is
> unthinkable apart from the surface on which it is laid out,
> so all our experience is not merely intermingled with the
> threats to human existence, but is constituted by them. It
> is what it is by its perilous nature. Therefore humanism
> does not substitute another certainty for the certainty of
> the gospels, nor another security for the security in God,
> nor another ultimate goal for eternal salvation. . . . It
> simply assumes the possibility of a significant life in trial

and error, with no other guarantee than man's inextinguishable endeavour, and without any otherworldly purposes.'[11]

There is no denying the unflinching integrity and deep courage of such a conception of man's existence. It is a persuasive representation of what, on reflection, appears to be the case. It is hard to conceive of, harder still (if not impossible) to imagine, a human existence which is not a seamless robe of joy and sorrow, laughter and tears, success and failure, life and death. Furthermore, it is true that in such a world man may hope to discover and construct oases of significance which offer him a temporary home in the desert which surrounds him. When disaster or tragedy strikes, there will always be some who rise to the heights of endurance and endeavour. They may grieve for a while and nurse their wounds. But then they are on the move again, determined to find another temporary human home. Or if they fall, there will be others to take their place. Life must go on. To speak to such of the consolations of religion is dangerously near mockery, to mouth the name of God almost an obscenity. There is no 'answer' to evil and death. They are the other side of good and life. They are ultimate facts, and they must be accepted as such.

What, then, shall we say of those believers who, when tragedy or disaster strikes, cry out to God in their anguish and in their pain entrust themselves and their broken world to his indefectible love and care? Are they deserting their human outpost in the face of the enemy, opting for comfort instead of courage, for fantasy instead of reality? Is it simply the case that they cannot endure the truth?

It could be so. In certain instances it almost certainly is so. Nor need we be too harsh with those with whom it is so. We do well to praise the courageous, but less well to condemn those unable to rise to the heights of courage. Nevertheless, it is not always and necessarily so. A hope that stems from faith in God does not always go hand in hand with a refusal to acknowledge worldly facts. A belief that these facts, evil and death, are not ultimate does not necessarily depend upon a denial of their all-too-real character as penultimate. Disaster remains disaster, and tragedy tragedy. There is no magic transformation which tears away a deceptive disguise and reveals a hidden character of secret blessing. The believer may have to confess that he has no completely convincing answer to the question how these things can be if the world is God's world. He has to hand no completely satisfactory theodicy. However, in perceiving and intending the world as God's world he refuses to take the present parameters of the world as ultimate. Its ultimate character has yet to be revealed. The story of the world is God's story as much as it is man's. More exactly it becomes man's story because it is first God's story. Thus what appears to the non-believer as clear evidence of the non-existence of God may become for the believer evidence rather of the penultimate 'absence' of God. And may not his 'absence' itself become a hidden and mysterious form of his presence?

> If I climb up into heaven, thou art there: if I go down to hell thou art there also. . . . The darkness is no darkness with thee, but the night is as clear as the day: the darkness and light to thee are both alike.[12]

When the light of God shines in the world's darkness, does it not, despite the darkness, shine unquenched? And when human hope is finally exhausted by the bounds of the world man knows too well, may it not be renewed in the God who appoints these bounds and who, in appointing, transcends them?

I have stretched and strained the ordinary uses of thought and language in an attempt to say something about a humanism which holds itself open to the transcendence of God. Such a humanism shares with its secular counterpart the belief that man is rooted in nature and shapes his humanity in history. It also shares a commitment to the drive to question, as one horizon gives place to another, and to the task of constructing a world in which human values may be nurtured and developed. It differs from its secular counterpart in that it sees this continuing movement and quest of the human spirit as a response to the initiating and concurrent movement and quest of the spirit of God.

In one sense, everything remains the same, for both Christian and secular humanist inhabit the same world.

> The only significant difference [writes Nathan Scott] that is established in the case of the Christian man has to do with his faith as to whence it is from which come the great gifts of courage and creativity and peace. . . . He lives in the historical order like all his fellows: the resource on which he relies is simply that particular hope and confidence to which he is given access in this world by reason of what he knows God to have done for this world. And, having this resource, his single vocation is to live, as did Jesus the Lord, in solicitude for, and in openness to, the man to whom he is related by the particular moment in history in which he happens to stand.[13]

In another sense, everything is different, for the 'same' world is focussed differently, and takes on a strange and unexpected significance. In ascribing its source, centre and goal to God the Christian humanist finds himself questioning whether his ordinary secular knowledge of the world is to be counted as 'knowledge' after all. Is the most important truth missing? Are the conditions which pre-scribe their own limits to his ordinary understanding robbed of their ultimacy and finality? Is the world itself to be 'understood' in terms of that which is not of the world? If God there be, then the history of the world is being made by God and man together. It is the history of two interactive freedoms operative in one and the same world. It is not pos-sible neatly to separate what is done by God and what is done by man. There is no absolute discontinuity which can be observed. The world is one, and for sense-perception there is only nature and man. God remains hidden, for he is not in the world as part of the world. He cannot be captured in the network of cause and effect. His presence in and to the world is not to be discerned by dispassionate observation of the world.

However, to say this is not to set the world over against God. Indeed, the Christian who affirms that God is Creator as well as Redeemer is bound to interpret the world in some sense or other as God's creative handiwork. There is no ab-solute discontinuity between nature and history. They are consecutive chapters in the same story. Nevertheless, it is first and foremost in relation to man himself, in the province of the exercise of his responsive and responsible freedom, that the presence of God declares itself to the believer. Of the various ways in which it is possible for him to perceive and intend the world, the Christian humanist affirms that it is most truly and adequately perceived and intended as God's world, communicating to him both the divine pressure and the divine call. And if it really is God's world, how may he not hope?

Man's responsive and responsible freedom—perhaps it is his reflection on the significance and implications of this mysterious characteristic of human existence which, more than anything else, prompts the half-believer seriously to entertain the possibility of the reality of God. For whence comes this ability so to respond? And to what is man being called to respond? He does not create his own freedom, but receives it as gift and invitation. Nor does he create his own values, but discovers them in open response to what is other than himself. Thus his search for significance and his commitment to truth and righteousness seem at one and the same time to rise out of the nature of things and finally to be contradicted by the nature of things. This contradiction may simply have to be faced and endured. There is no necessary connection between what is and what ought to be. Indeed, as things are in the world as it is, much that is ought not to be and much that ought to be is not. Nevertheless, the contradiction poses a threat to human hope and endeavour. At the root of such hope and endeavour is to be found a basic and pervasive attitude of trust—trust that the open and responsive way of life is not futile and pointless.

Although this basic attitude is not tied to any specific expectation, and so is not immediately contradicted by the disappointment of that particular expectation, it can nevertheless be called in question. Particular disappointments may become so many or so intense that the basic attitude itself is placed in jeopardy. Is it madness and folly? Ought one to adopt a more 'realistic' view of life's potentialities? Is the 'reasonable' moral policy one of paying some, but not too much, attention to the call of neighbour and the future, and of concentrating on the furtherance of one's own individual interests—a policy of enlightened self-interest?

It is not surprising that many who find themselves moving beyond a policy of enlightened self-interest also find themselves drawn towards a faith that their venture runs with the deep grain of things and is upheld by an ultimate and universal power which is utterly trustworthy. Such a faith can certainly provide psychological support in times of testing. But is it anything more than a 'noble lie'? It sounds as if the believer is saying that what he would dearly like to be the case must be the case, or that even if it is not the case it is expedient to imagine that it is the case. But belief may not act only in this simple and supportive way. It may also penetrate more deeply into the manner and matter of the believer's response, correcting, shaping and transforming his attitudes and actions. One's way of life and one's religious beliefs cannot be kept carefully apart. Nor do the latter simply provide a psychological support for the former. They may come to specify, as well as to support, the way of life, and to determine the content which is to be given to an open response to neighbour and the future. It might appear at first glance, for example, that one could choose to follow the way of Jesus because it embodied the truly good and human way, while rejecting Jesus' own faith that his way was an obedient response to the calling of his heavenly Father. But would this, on reflection, be seen to do full justice to this way of life? Might it not be a failure seriously to grasp and grapple with it, were it construed as anything less than a lived response to the divine initiative? Was it not a statement in life and death, not only about man, but also about God? And if a statement about God, was it a true statement?

The half-believer, I have said, holds in mind the *possibility* of the reality of God. He is a half-believer precisely because the immediate certainty of God has vanished from his consciousness. It is neither a self-evident truth that God exists nor an undeniable fact of his own experience. But the way of Jesus, and the person of Jesus, continue to exercise a persistent claim on his allegiance. He wills to be his disciple and to follow his way, even though he cannot fully understand, and is unable fully to accept as his own, Jesus' fundamental faith in the reality of God. He cannot accept, because it is not within his own choice either to affirm or to deny. Belief is not a matter of choosing, it waits on the evidence. For the time being he can only hope in God. However, the 'evidence' may involve and include a change of perspective, a new vision, a conversion of the mind. The venture of discipleship and the apprenticeship of prayer may themselves lead to that conversion and conviction which together constitute the perception of faith. He may come to believe. There are times, indeed, when he already 'believes', and he discerns patterns in his experience and in the world around him which confirm and strengthen his belief. At other times, however, the patterns are broken, belief is shaken, and the emptiness and the doubt recur. But should he be dismayed? Is there not still the shadow of a presence? Will the very loss of the sense of the transcendent, if patiently accepted and faithfully endured, through a kind of 'negative capability', bring him deeper into the heart of the sustaining Mystery? Does the emptiness, too, belong to God? Does the Creator make room for his creation?

5

THE WAY OF JESUS

Simon Peter answered him, 'Lord, to whom shall we
go? You have the words of eternal life.'   (John 6.68)

Once in a while there crosses the stage of history a man
whose life and teaching challenge and transform our human
consciousness. After him things are never quite the same
again. He has given us a new conception of what it is, or of
what it could be, to exercise our humanity. Our self-
understanding has been called into question. Such a man
was Jesus of Nazareth.

To speak in this way is, admittedly, to use a very different
idiom from that of traditional Christian proclamation.
Such proclamation about Jesus is first and foremost a proclamation about God. The story of Jesus is part of the story
of God. The role which Jesus fulfilled was not that of a mere
man among men, nor was it his bare humanity which gives
him his ultimate and eternal significance. The latter derives,
on the contrary, from the role which he fulfils in the econ-
omy of divine salvation. The unique Son of his heavenly
Father, he is sent by God into the world to redeem the
world. When his earthly mission is completed on the cross,
where men have nailed and set him at naught, he is raised by

God from the dead and exalted into heaven, where he reigns at the right hand of his Father until all things shall be subjected to the divine will in judgement and restoration.

Nothing, however, in this traditional Christian proclamation prevents our asking what manner of man this Jesus was. Indeed, the story itself seems to invite just such a question, for the Son carries in himself the express image of his Father; and unless we arbitrarily restrict this image to certain aspects of the person of Jesus, and deny it to others, so destroying the unity and continuity which belong to an integrated human life, our attention must be drawn not only to his crucifixion and resurrection, however central these events must be for understanding the claim that he conquered sin and death, but also to the life he lived and to the beliefs by which he lived. To make the same point in a different way, it was not just *any* man who was crucified and raised from the dead, it was *Jesus of Nazareth*. The significance of his death and resurrection is bound up with the significance of his life. Thus to ask what manner of man he was is an intrinsic part of any determined attempt to grasp the meaning of the whole Christian story and proclamation.

To ask the question, 'What manner of man?' is one thing; to offer a firm and assured answer is another. There are scholars who tell us that practically nothing can be known for certain about the life and teaching of Jesus. It may well be true that they overstate their case, setting up criteria for 'certainty' far more stringent than those accepted in general by historians in other fields. However, the considerations which prompt their agnosticism cannot be ignored. The gospels which provide us with almost all our evidence of the life and teaching of Jesus cannot simply be taken at their face value. They reflect, more or less, the particular points of view of their writers. The traditions on which they are based have already undergone a process of selection and shaping for use by the early Christian Church, and in this process a clear distinction does not always appear to have been preserved between the memory of Jesus and the experience of the risen Christ. Such considerations render the task of recovering the exact teaching of Jesus, especially his teaching about himself, and the precise course of his life, exceedingly difficult. But we are not condemned to total agnosticism. As J. L. Houlden remarks:

> there is no logic which could lead us to believe that of four accounts of a man's teaching all are equally remote from the truth or that, even if all four express distinctive views of him, he is thereby rendered totally obscure to us. It may be that he did not speak precisely so and so, but that nevertheless the thrust of his message was thus and thus.[1]

Something, then, concerning what I shall call *the way of Jesus* can, I believe, with reasonable confidence be affirmed. In speaking of the way of Jesus I shall not be referring to the particular course of his ministry, nor to the detailed interpretation of his individual sayings. Rather I shall have in mind the fundamental perspective and orientation of his life —the ultimate horizon within which he perceived the world around him and which gave it its predominant significance, and the direction and quality of his response to the people and situations which he encountered in that world.

What then was Jesus' fundamental perspective? I suggest that he saw the world as *God's world,* and this with an immediacy and intensity of vision that overshadowed all else, making the distant one present, bringing God to earth. He proclaimed the kingdom of God. What precisely he intended by this proclamation is a matter of dispute, and more than one interpretation is possible. Both the nature of this kingdom and the time and manner of its coming are uncertain. To what extent Jesus himself used the language of Jewish apocalyptic and what significance he gave to it are likewise uncertain. More often than not he spoke of it in parables. It was like a pearl of great price, or seed-time and harvest. What may, however, be said without much fear of contradiction is that for Jesus the one inescapable and over-riding fact of the world was the fact of God himself, and that the recognition of this fact by man was a matter of extreme urgency, a matter of life and death. Furthermore, although this sense of urgency may have found expression from time to time in language of judgement and condemnation, God was utterly gracious, utterly loving and utterly trustworthy. He willed to bless rather than to curse, to give life rather than to condemn to death. Jesus knew him as a heavenly Father and addressed him as 'Abba'. Contrasted with the proclamation of John the Baptist, which sounded as warning and threat, his own proclamation was good news, for the God whom he proclaimed, a God of boundless if holy love, was a ground of faith and a source of hope.

Such a fundamental perspective determined the orientation of Jesus' whole life. As son of a heavenly Father he expressed his Father's attitude to the world, calling men to share his own perspective and orientation, for his Father was also their Father. As God was gracious and loving, so he was gracious and loving; so too would his disciples be gracious and loving. The man for God, he was for that very reason the man for men. The two great commandments which summed up the Law were part and parcel of one and the same response to which his teaching was a summons. God's love for man signified that no man was without value, no man was beyond the pale, except in so far as he might reject the gracious claims of the divine love and so put himself beyond the pale. So Jesus came to be known as a friend pre-eminently of publicans and sinners; those who were counted by the righteous as beyond the pale. This love of men took note only of their needs, not least their need of forgiveness and renewal, and to these needs he ministered, neither jealous of his own reputation nor fearful lest the company he kept might imperil his own standing with God. Reflecting the indiscriminate love of God he himself loved indiscriminately, caring not for himself but for those to whom his Father willed to give his kingdom. In short, we may say that Jesus chose the way of sacrificial love— although it is patently absurd to think that we can adequately specify this way in a single phrase, a way which took a life and a death to spell out in full.

One feature of the way of Jesus requires special attention. He seems deliberately to have refused to be drawn into the area of human claims and counter-claims. He did not set himself up as a judge among men. It is this fact, perhaps more than anything else, which has made it practically impossible to apply his teaching directly to the solution of those problems in human life which stem from the conflict of interests and in which the careful balance of claim and counter-claim plays an essential role. Christians have devised various ways of accommodating their own involvement in human affairs to this impossibility. They have, for example, distinguished between the universal precepts of Jesus and his counsels of perfection; or between the twofold rule of God, with his right hand in the kingdom of Christ and with his left hand in the kingdoms of the world. However, Jesus simply did not concern himself with matters of human justice. For justice is tied to desert and is essentially backward-looking. But Jesus was forward-looking, concerned with what men might become rather than with what they had been. He looked to their needs rather than to their deserts, and from his God-centred perspective it was clear to him that even the most deserving were only unprofitable servants. What man lacked, however, it was God's will freely to give. From this perspective the nicely calculated processes of balancing claim and counter-claim were beside the point. They stemmed from self-assertion and self-justification, and embodied a perspective on human life the assumed validity of which was precisely what Jesus challenged.

For him the love of neighbour recognised no limits either to its demands or to its sphere of action. In Matthew's account, when Peter, catching something of his Master's teaching, but still operating within the bounds of justifiable claims, asked him how often he should forgive his brother, and suggested that seven times might be the most that could be expected, Jesus answered 'Not seven times, but seventy times seven.' From the perspective of God forgiveness knows no limits; times are without number. In Luke's account, when asked to define one's neighbour, whom the Law commanded a man to love as himself, Jesus told the parable of the Good Samaritan, and thereby turned the question upside down; for the parable illustrates and expresses neighbourly love towards anyone in need and the questioner is bidden to go and do likewise. Love is not due to a neighbour because the neighbour belongs to a definite and limited category of human beings, the defining characteristic of which constitutes the source of the claim on another's love. Rather the neighbour belongs to no or to every category, he is anyone in need; and neighbourly love is rooted in the will to meet another's need, not in the acknowledgement of a claim established apart from that need. The way of sacrificial love is unreserved and uncalculating, outward-looking and self-forgetful, responsible and responsive, and always open to new and creative possibilities.

Because perspective and orientation were completely integrated with each other, Jesus' life and teaching revealed a striking unity. Not only did he teach the way of sacrificial love, he also lived it. His life was a commentary on his teaching, and his teaching was a verbal articulation of the horizons of his life. Since this was so, he seemed to many so different from their scribes and teachers of the Law. The latter appealed to an authority outside themselves, and often alien to themselves; whereas the authority of Jesus was somehow internal to himself and bound up with his own personal being. He *had* authority, an authority which derived from another source than any which could be traced to the recognised and duly accredited training in the school of the Law. It is not possible to speak here with certainty, but it is not unlikely that it was the question of the nature of his authority which brought him into conflict with the religious leaders of his people and finally led to his death. We cannot be certain what Jesus' attitude to the Law was. From the gospel records it seems that at times he intensified its demands, at other times ignored them. Much, if not all, of his moral teaching could be understood as an interpretation rather than a rejection of the Law. He sought to recover its original intention which had disappeared under the detailed rules of the tradition. He was not concerned with a detailed casuistry which could be applied to men who were 'so unteachable'.[2] He set about teaching the unteachable. He challenged the assumptions which underlay the casuistry, and in so challenging he was not unwilling to appeal to the Law itself. The records which we have show that there was an apparent ambiguity in Jesus' attitude to the Law. If we wish, then, to understand the reasons for his condemnation by the religious authorities and his being sentenced to death,[3] we shall be closer to the truth if we cease to look for any specific item of his teaching which could be seen clearly to be against the Law, and fasten our attention rather on the matter of his authority. He taught in the first person. In so doing he appeared to be setting himself above the Law. Since the Law was God's Law, this could be construed only as 'blasphemy'. Thus he constituted a threat to the whole religious tradition which understood the Law as the fundamental and pre-eminent medium through which God had communicated his will to his chosen people. It is in this sense that Jesus could be judged as being 'against' the Law; and it is in this sense that we can understand Kurt Niederwimmer's conclusion that 'Jesus stands over against the whole sacred tradition of his people, the written as well as the oral, with an astonishing sovereign independence and inner freedom.'[4] Who is this man in whom teaching and living are integrated in an immediacy of experience and authority?

It has been suggested that the nature of Jesus' life-work can be illuminated by the analogy of healing.[5] The healer's prime and predominant concern is with the health of his patient. There may be other interests which as a scientist or as a citizen he properly recognises, but these must not be allowed to affect his professional ethic as a healer. Within that ethic it is the patient's interest that matters. That is the one thing that counts above all else. Now:

> 'in the gospels Christ is presented throughout as the healer. And this healing is not regarded as an accidental feature of his work; it is not even an essential accompaniment to the work. It *is* the work. What Jesus does for people's bodies is part and parcel of what he does for their souls. . . . To the first Christians there is no doubt

that the healing work of Jesus was not merely a kind of parable of his atoning work (though it *was* that), but an actual demonstration of it.'[6]

Jesus was concerned not with the alleviation of the symptoms of disease, but with the healing of the disease itself. For him the roots of the disease lay in a defective perception of God. So he set about healing the 'unhealable' and teaching the 'unteachable'. He proclaimed the forgiveness of sins. He was the forgiveness of sins. He summoned to repentance, to a radical change of perspective, and he made such repentance a living possibility. In such a work of healing lay the ground of his 'professional' ethic. Other interests proper to the whole context of human life with its claims and counter-claims there might be; but because of his concentration on his own work of healing, a concentration which arose from his belief that in man's relation to God lay the single ultimate source of all human health and sickness rather than from any narrow and self-appointed 'professionalism', he gave such interests and the moral problems which they engendered little or no attention. Indeed, attention to such interests might simply exacerbate and prolong the sickness, for it could conceal the need for a radical change of perspective and a thorough re-orientation of life.

If the matter of Jesus' teaching and the manner of his living expressed and embodied the way of sacrificial love, so too did the encompassing of his dying. It was an extension of the mode of his life into the mode of his death. We may understand it first and foremost as the final and irrevocable statement of his chosen way of life. Life and death were of a piece in a single integrity of action and passion. As he lived, so he died, without deflecting from the cause which he had set himself. In the context of personal integrity we can interpret his death as a testimony.

> It is the statement of a certain set of values, the values for which and by which he lived. It is a statement of the supreme importance of those values, that he will die rather than compromise them, die in order to express them. Jesus came to force men to respond. They did; some by killing him; some by attaching themselves to him, living for what he had lived for, and in some cases dying as he had died. Jesus had no guarantee that the appeal he made in dying would be understood or heeded. He had no guarantee that anything he stood for would survive his death. His death is a statement of faith, and a statement made in faith.[7]

In this context of personal integrity we may go on to speak of Jesus' victory in death. In the hour of his own greatest need he refused to desert to the enemy, but followed the way of sacrificial love to the very end. The immediacy of his sense of the presence of God may have been obscured. That such immediacy was in fact obscured is suggested by the reported episode in the Garden of Gethsemane, although the authenticity of this episode is problematic if his disciples slept while he prayed. (One does not usually recount to others the content of one's deepest prayers.) However, the clouding over of his immediate sense of God, if such occurred, strengthened rather than weakened his will. Having set his hands to the plough he could not now look back. If the way of sacrificial love led him to a cross, to a cross he must go. His love persisted even in death.

In the context of personal integrity there is nothing more that needs to be said. But is this context adequate? What are we to say of the faith in God to which such integrity was a response? What of Jesus' complete trust in the utter graciousness of God, who was a God of the living and not of the dead? Christian proclamation does not end at the moment of Jesus' death. It speaks of a victory, not only in death, but also over death. God did not leave the dead Jesus to suffer corruption in the grave, but raised him on the third day to life in heaven. What are we to say concerning such a proclamation?

I shall return to this question in a later lecture. Here I would only observe that the 'resurrection' of Jesus is not to be understood as a 'proof' of the divine presence and activity, in any sense of 'proof' which would stand up to scrutiny in an historian's study or in a court of law. It is not a fact of history that can be placed beyond reasonable doubt. It may not be lacking in evidence of one sort or another, but it remains in the area of faith. All that I wish to affirm here and now is that the resurrection faith of the early Church led them to see the death of Jesus in a new and strange light. The cross did not signify the abandonment of Jesus by God. Nor did it demonstrate that, despite his personal integrity, Jesus was deluded in his fundamental perspective by which he perceived and intended the world as God's world. Rather, resurrection-faith suggested that the death of Jesus itself might be seen as a divine vindication of the way of sacrificial love. Even the cross was in some mysterious and barely explicable way an instrument of divine grace, the meeting-place of mercy and truth. This strange light colours all the New Testament accounts and interpretations of Jesus' death. It is most striking in the Fourth Gospel, in which the cross itself is presented as a throne of glory, and God is present in his holiness and love, accompanying Jesus through the time of his dying. Thus Jesus' death becomes more than the statement of a man, written in blood and moulded by the forces of human integrity. It is also a statement of God, in which death is subsumed into life and despair gives place to hope.

Confronted with the way of Jesus, acknowledging its power to awaken his deepest human insights and to evoke his allegiance, yet at the same time conscious of the distance between the experienced world of Jesus and that of himself, and apprehensive of a certain strangeness, perhaps even of unreality, attaching to the gospel story, how shall the half-believer respond?

He can, perhaps, put in brackets the fundamental perspective of Jesus and yet subscribe to his teaching of the human centrality of sacrificial love. He will then regard Jesus in the light of a profound moral teacher, who had seen with blinding and consistent clarity what lesser men had glimpsed intermittently and confusedly. Sacrificial love is the normative criterion of human flourishing. It requires no divine justification, for it accords with human nature and reflects man's deepest tendency, attempts to deny which are tragic and ultimately self-defeating.[8] It binds together the origins and the goals of a truly human life. It finds its full expression both in friendship and in justice. It generates a social as well as an individual ethic.

Such a response deserves deep respect. Unbelievers as well as believers have acknowledged the claims of sacrificial love, the value of persons as persons, apart from their attainments and merits, and the special duty of the strong to protect and aid the weak. There is certainly a wide overlap between the way of Jesus and the way of many a religious agnostic, even if the shared language of love may tend to conceal certain subtle but important differences. Nevertheless, without Jesus' fundamental perspective the way of sacrificial love may lose its centrality and stability. There are those who have denied that it is the norm of human flourishing. Some men are inferior as men, and to extend to them the regard which one might reasonably extend to others is sentimentality or even injustice. Or again, even if the way of Jesus is valid as a noble ideal, it nevertheless remains an impossible ideal. Individual and group egoism is so deeply entrenched in existing human nature and culture, whatever may be said on the other side concerning man's 'deepest tendency' to love, that claim and counter-claim must be regulated by law and controlled by force. A balance of power is likely to achieve more for the total human good than indiscriminate love. An appeal to enlightened self-interest has more chance of success than any appeal to the example of Jesus. It is sometimes said that, if only man lived and loved as Jesus lived and loved, there would be universal peace and happiness. This may or may not be the case. It is at least arguable that love itself cannot solve all human conflicts, but that love also requires wisdom and competence, virtues of a practical and technical kind. Be that as it may. 'If only men followed the way of Jesus. . . .' But that is no answer to human ills. It is simply another way of stating the problem. Either men will not or else they cannot. The egoism in men's hearts is too deep to be changed by moral exhortation. What is needed is an experience which restructures their fundamental perspective and orientation.

Thus the half-believer is moved to consider a second possibility.[9] The emphasis now is not on moral idealism but on the restructuring of human experience. What the way of Jesus offers is the experience of creative growth. This involves a sudden and non-logical perceptual shift, a change in the way in which a man sees himself and his world. The old self-centred perception has led to intolerable contradictions in human life. A new perception needs to take its place, an experience of liberation from the old self leading to an openness to life and the future and to an outwardness of concern for others. The old egoism, with its self-concern and self-protectiveness, yields to a new self-forgetfulness. Even anxiety concerning one's own salvation is now forgotten. 'One is challenged to move beyond himself in concern for others and in openness to further change. The Christian gospel is not presented as a lifesaver. Rather, it involves a positive mandate to live for others.'[10]

That such experiences can and do occur in response to the gospel of Jesus is not to be disputed. They cannot be engineered by a deliberate act of the will. Penitence, in the sense of a moral repudiation of the past self, can only prepare for their occurrence. They are gift and grace. They are like a rebirth or a resurrection.

> The prelude to resurrection [writes Harry Williams] as we experience it in this life is always powerlessness. We cannot raise ourselves by our own boot-strings. . . . Our experience of resurrection in this life has been the result of miracle. When here and now we have known ourselves raised from the dead, we have in that experience apprehended ourselves as being somehow created by a power which is beyond us . . . a power which for want of a better description we have called the Eternal Word.[11]

Such, then, is the experience of creative growth that can come from the gospel of Jesus, though it can come from other sources as well. But what of the language in which Jesus experienced his own insight and vision? What of God and his kingdom? In so far as the substance of Christian experience is affirmed to be an individual's creative growth, the language and ideas by which this growth is promoted and in which it is expressed are only of secondary importance. Thus:

> The Christian is called to commitment but not to any ideology. He is not called to be committed to the idea of a triune God, a risen Christ, or even the man Jesus. Rather, his commitment is to a *growth process* in the direction of *responsible action* expressed in increased concern for others and openness to future change.[12]

Language about God and his kingdom is functional rather than informative. It facilitates the breakdown of the old perceptive structures and the appearance of the new. In so far as it does this, it serves its purpose; if it fails to do this, it is dispensable. A theology which objectifies such language into statements about a supernatural being and a supernatural world is misconceived. It mistakes creative fiction for prosaic, if supernatural, fact.

This second approach to an interpretation and appropriation of the way of Jesus promises to be more fruitful than the first. It incorporates the latter's emphasis on concern for others and self-forgetful regard for their needs and potentialities, but it sees such an attitude as rising out of a new perception and as a response to a transforming experience. Nevertheless, it is not without its own difficulties. If language about God and his kingdom have only functional validity, then the criteria of its proper functioning must be provided by the concepts of 'growth' and 'responsible action'. But what is to count as growth, and what as responsible action? Concern for others may well be accepted as one criterion—'by their fruits ye shall know them'—but is it a sufficient criterion? What form is such concern to take? Again, openness to future change may be another criterion—'we do not yet know what we shall become'—but not every change is necessarily a change for the better. Love demands fidelity and stability as well as sensitivity to new challenges and opportunities. Ideas of what constitutes creative growth and responsible action are not easily separable from beliefs about the nature and destiny of man. Furthermore, for Jesus himself God was surely something immeasurably more than a functionally valid idea. He was the central reality of his experience, the recipient of his love and obedience, the sustaining ground of his action and the source and goal of his hope. We may conclude, if we must, that in all this Jesus was mistaken. It is quite another matter to suggest that there was nothing after all for him to be mistaken about. Jesus lived from God and towards God. This faith not only gave rise to his concern for others and his openness to the future, it also penetrated deeply into their innermost structure and content. It determined the full range and nature of his present love and his future hope.

So the half-believer moves on to consider yet a third possibility, namely, that the power which raises a man from death in this life, creating a new perspective and orientation, is not one power among many which from time to time affect in striking and unexpected ways a man's perception of himself and his world, a power which 'for want of a better description' we call 'the Eternal Word'. Rather, it *is* the Eternal Word, by which all things are created, sustained and drawn towards their fulfilment. No doubt the language that we use to speak of this Eternal Word, and the concepts in which we attempt to articulate our understanding, remain more or less inadequate. Theology is not an exact science. But together with the experience of resurrection there arise a vision and a hope, and these go hand in hand with an affirmation that, whatever else is true about the world in which we live, it is ultimately such that our vision and hope are well-grounded. We move 'beyond' narrowly empirical discourse about the way the world goes and find ourselves beginning to speak about 'God'. In so speaking we give our language more than a functional and finally dispensable validity, for 'God' is now the supreme and determining reality of the world.

As we have already seen, men raise questions about the ultimate nature of things and the meaning of life, questions which can be dismissed as meaningless but which nevertheless persistently recur. In the midst of time they create some picture of things which links together past, present and future. Some pictures are more coherent and more persuasive than others. The fact remains that they find themselves confronted with ambiguities. There seems to be a continuing conflict of opposites within the experienced structures of existence—good and evil, freedom and bondage, light and darkness. Now one, now the other of these opposites predominates. So men oscillate between love and fear, joy and grief, hope and despair. Obviously in such a world men need to have courage. Can they also find confidence and trust?

Is it possible that these ambiguities are themselves somehow containable and contained within a reality which is always creative and always trustworthy? Does God reign, even if the language expressing his kingship is of necessity symbolic and imprecise, pointing as best it can to that which is ultimate and mysterious, but nevertheless holy and gracious? Was such the faith which made Jesus the man he was, and determined the way he went? And was that way a testing of that faith to the breaking-point? And is the Christian proclamation about Jesus and his resurrection, whatever else it may be, a recurrent and persistent conviction that the 'breaking-point'—for such it seemed to the eyes of many— was itself a new beginning, no less than an 'act of God'?

87

Was, then, the whole life of Jesus, was Jesus himself, an 'act of God', and does he enable us to apprehend and respond to 'God's eternal activity'?

> Whatever else the Gospel may mean, all we can be sure of is that it means that it is possible for men to break out of the selfishness, the self-deceit, the arrogance which encrusts their lives and to live more selflessly, justly, honestly, and lovingly because they are confident that the whatever-it-is that underlies our existence, that gives and puts limits to our lives, is Holy and Good beyond all thought and imagination; that in the presence of this mystery all humanly accepted excellences, those things in which men put their confidence and trust, are childish. . . .
>
> The Christian does not know how or why this transformation of vision occurs when he no longer trusts in himself and lives in relation to the mystery. . . . He tries to grasp intellectually what has happened to him but it eludes his comprehension and understanding. Sometimes he doubts. All he can say for sure is that things seem different from what they once seemed and that they can also seem different to others and that this is Good News, a basis for hope. Hence, he becomes a steward of this mystery.[13]

Jesus not only proclaimed the mystery. He embodied and communicated the mystery. The centre of his own identity lay in the heart of the mystery. This authority was not his own, but the authority of the one whom he addressed as 'Father'. The words he uttered were a word from God. Was he himself, in some way, a Word of God, the Father's beloved Son?

6

THE KINGDOM OF GOD

'Thy kingdom come.'   (Matt. 6.10)

The life, teaching and death of Jesus may be read as a statement about man. The way of life is the way of sacrificial
love. It draws a man out of himself into the world and
towards his neighbour. It is calling and gift, a new perspective and orientation, before it is achievement. A man's life
does not consist in what he possesses in and for himself, but
in what he becomes in creative response to and in co-
operation with that which is other than himself, not least his
neighbour. For example, in giving and receiving between
man and man my neighbour's needs become my needs and
my needs become his needs. There occur an enlargement
and interpenetration of personal concern, a responsibility
and a responsiveness, a freedom in interdependence. The
opposite of such love is traditionally said to be pride, or selfishness. But such selfishness may also be said to have its
roots in fear, fear of what is other than myself when that
other is such as to disturb and threaten an initial and basic
attitude of trust. Such fear shuts me in on myself, circum-
scribes the world in which I feel at home, and prompts me to
erect protective barriers between myself and my neighbour.

I endeavour to establish my world over against his world. My neighbour becomes my enemy, the object of my hatred as well as of my fear. So hatred begets hatred and the circle of destructiveness is complete. Only forgiveness, acceptance and reconciliation can hope to break out of the circle and to restore the way of life. Only a perfect love can cast out fear.

In its purity, intensity and boundlessness the way of Jesus may be reckoned as a noble but impossible ideal. Nevertheless it has certain analogues in our own experience. It awakens echoes. We know what it is to experience renewal, integration and enhancement from a source and power beyond our egocentric selves. Such experiences come to us as gift and grace, sometimes with a suddenness and unexpectedness such as to constitute a kind of rebirth, or resurrection. The old self dies and a new self comes to life. At other times the discontinuity is less apparent. A pattern of growth begins to establish itself. Continuities occur. Even so, the pattern is one of openness and outwardness, a giving and a losing of oneself to receive and find oneself anew. It is almost a commonplace in our contemporary understanding of the psychodynamics of human growth to stress the central importance of love and trust for the development of a responsible and responsive personality. I am a person, not because I am a thinking being, but because I am a responding being, and I become a responding being because I am lured into responsibility. I count as someone because I count to someone. In being given to myself through the love of another I can then become free to give myself to another in love. Because the world as I have first experienced it in and through my parents has been gracious and trustworthy, I have been given a basic confidence which enables me to respond creatively to the ever-expanding and certainly less secure world around me.

For most of us, however, if not for all, such precious experiences of gift and grace are all too fleeting and fragile. Our acquired dispositions are far from being consistently open, loving and free from fear and anxiety. There is much within ourselves as well as in the spheres of nature and history which militates against the way of life which Jesus followed. Experiences of growth in trust, hope and love occur within a larger context which remains ambiguous. Is 'that which underlies our existence, that gives and puts limits to our lives, Holy and Good beyond all thought and imagination',[1] or is it cruelly indifferent? We oscillate between belief and unbelief, between trust and suspicion, between hope and despair, between love and fear. Is the way of Jesus an inviting but in the end a blind alley? Are his words of light and life a cry of protest in the prevailing night? Or are they what believers have always claimed them to be, an Eternal Word stemming from God himself, the only adequate response to a Love that moves the stars?

As we have already remarked, more often than not men have nourished their ideals and aspirations with the faith that they are ultimately grounded in 'the nature of things'. As Langdon Gilkey has put it:

There are facets of what we have called 'common grace' known everywhere in human existence, i.e., everywhere where a human life or a community of men vividly experiences on the secular level the meaning and creativity of their own particularity. But when men become aware, through the relativity of what they do, and through the uncertainties of the historical context within which these activities must function, of the fragility of all their meanings, and stare at this Void, then only the awareness of an unconditioned context of meaning, of a purpose or telos in events that is not fragile and that transcends even what they come to love, can put meaning back into life. And thus arise both the idolatries of secular existence and its own deeper search for the reality of what we call 'God'.[2]

Now it may be the case that the search for God is doomed to failure because there is no God, and that the idea of a 'concordance of beginning, middle and end'[3] is a dream which vanishes in the clear light of day, when the gods are shown to be the idols which they always were. The secular powers of nature and history afford no 'unconditioned context of meaning'. Neither evolution nor revolution establishes a sure and certain hope. Nor can man trust himself to make the dream come true. So much is common ground to believer and unbeliever. 'Religious people have never denied, indeed they affirm, that God means to kill us all in the end, and in the end He is going to succeed.'[4] Yet the dream persists. 'We must dream.'[5] The dream expresses a fundamental movement of the human spirit. Where there is no vision, the people perish. But the believer has been vouchsafed a vision. For him the shadows of a human dream have given place to the substance of a divine act. In Jesus the light has shone in the darkness, the light of eternal day, and the dream has been transformed into reality, not dissipated into nothingness, for God has visited and redeemed his people. How might these things be?

What for many of his religious contemporaries remained a distant dream was for Jesus the basis of his life and teaching. His way of sacrificial love sprang from the immediacy of his heavenly Father's presence, a Father whose indiscriminate and boundless love was evident in creation and who desired to give good things to all who asked. In this immediacy of experience Jesus proclaimed the Kingdom of God and prayed for its coming. Both prayer and proclamation were characterised by the same immediacy. God's kingdom was no longer a distant dream; it was at hand, within men's grasp. There was no time for careful observation and calculated prediction, which pushed back the kingdom into a receding future. It was already harvest-time. To the perceptive eye of faith signs of the coming kingdom were already to be discerned: the kingdom itself could not long be delayed. Thus in the immediacy of Jesus' experience there were both present and future dimensions. Faith and hope were united. We may speak either of his faith in the presence of the coming God, or of his hope in the coming of the present God. Perhaps it is a mistake to attempt to speak more precisely. The evidence may be taken to suggest that Jesus looked forward to a time within the span of his own generation when the powers of evil would be decisively and finally overthrown and the divine peace and righteousness would embrace both heaven and earth. On the other hand, we must reckon with the fact that the 'time' which characterises the prophetic vision is not to be identified straightforwardly with historical time. It was precisely the calculations of historical time which Jesus rejected when asked about the kingdom's coming. Even so, he looked forward confidently and expectantly to the future. His whole manner of life and teaching was the outcome of his obedience to the present and coming God, who provided human existence with its ultimate horizon, and who thus gave it its meaning and would give it its fulfilment.

Were this faith and hope by which Jesus lived misplaced? It might indeed appear so. He died a criminal's death on a cross, while the world continued along its old ways. Where, then, was the expected kingdom of righteousness and peace? The believer answers that it is not yet, for he still looks, and prays in Jesus' own words, for its coming. What, then, is it that sustains his hope? Is it anything more than the persistence of an age-old dream? To this the believer replies that his hope is sustained, not as a dream, but by the Christian proclamation that God raised Jesus from the dead and exalted him to his right hand on high. Hence the way of Jesus was not simply the product of a human dream, it was also a divine self-disclosure. It was as much a statement of God as it was the statement of a man. God himself had validated the faith of Jesus and had confirmed his hope.

That God raised Jesus from the dead has sometimes been acclaimed by the Christian enthusiast as the best attested fact of history. How else, it is said, could one adequately account for the origin of the Christian Church?[6] However, this will not do. We may admit that there would have been no Christian Church had there not been a firm belief in the resurrection of Jesus from the dead, for such a belief was and always has been a constitutive and determining feature of its proclamation and hence of its *raison d'être*. But the justification of this belief is another question. The extraordinariness of the belief certainly seems to demand some sort of explanation; but to argue that the belief was so extraordinary that only the actuality of Jesus' resurrection could account for it is unconvincing. Men do come to hold extraordinary beliefs for no good reason at all, and some of these beliefs are remarkably persistent and influential, sometimes for better, sometimes for worse.

I have neither the time nor the ability to give to this whole topic the attention that it properly deserves, but the following considerations seem to me to suggest strongly that for us today, whatever the situation may have been for the early 'witnesses to the resurrection', belief in the resurrection of Jesus must remain a matter of belief, a possibility and maybe even something of a hope, rather than a matter of knowledge.

First, let us consider the question of historical evidence. Let us assume, for the sake of argument, that some of the disciples of Jesus, and others who had not been his disciples, had visual and auditory experiences after his death which they took to be experiences of Jesus as again alive; and, further, that there are no compelling reasons, such as might be adduced from our knowledge of other somewhat analogous experiences, for classifying these experiences as hallucinatory. Let us also assume—though this is more debatable—that the traditions of an empty tomb withstand critical analysis and may be taken as solid evidence that there was an empty tomb. What follows?

In the case of the empty tomb a variety of explanations might be offered, and the gospel records themselves suggest that explanations were in fact offered other than that to which the early Christians subscribed. The body of Jesus might not have been buried in a tomb. Or it might have been removed from the tomb. Or the empty tomb might not have been the tomb of Jesus. It might in principle be possible to show that these alternative explanations are unlikely. But are they *more* unlikely than the explanation that Jesus was raised from the dead? It may be retorted that the unlikeliness of the alternative considerations stems from strictly historical considerations, while the 'unlikeliness' of Jesus' resurrection is based on *a priori* grounds. So be it. But these *a priori* grounds are not simply arbitrary. They 'fit' much if not all of our experience, and they require unusually strong empirical evidence if they are to be confidently rejected. Is not the historian bound to say concerning the empty tomb 'I believe this rather than that for this and that reason, but the evidence is far from conclusive'?

In the case of the visual and auditory experiences, even though these may be more central to the tradition than the story of the empty tomb, the position is even less clear. Granted that they occurred, were they rightly taken, i.e. interpreted, albeit immediately and unconsciously, as experiences of Jesus as again alive? To test this interpretation the historian would properly look for confirming evidence outside the experiences themselves. If Jesus were alive again, then this or that might be expected to be the case. But no such extra-experiential evidence is forthcoming. The experiences as such suggest no further predictions which might confirm or refute their interpretation. They are, so to speak, self-contained.

> The witnesses make it clear that the visibility, audibility and tangibility of the risen Jesus coincided exactly in time and space with their experiences of the risen Jesus: that is, the witnesses were not able, and did not intend to be able when asked, 'What do you mean, "risen"?' to say: 'Look over there and you will observe such-and-such happening . . . The witnesses speak precisely of appearances, not of meetings. But then there *can* have been no occurrences other than the occurrence of the experiences of the witnesses themselves, of which trace might now be found in the sources.[7]

Thus the historian, *qua* historian, finds himself in an impasse. For if he argues that there is no evidence outside the experiences themselves to show that the interpretation of the experiences was in fact correct—for example, that non-believers saw the risen Jesus, or that he left some material evidence of his activity which could not possibly have originated in the days before his death—the believer is likely to reply that evidence *of that kind* is not to be expected, for

Jesus is not alive again with *that kind of life*.

This brings us to our second set of considerations, viz. concerning the meaning of the claim that God raised Jesus from the dead. The new life of Jesus was not the old life restored; it was life in glory. The claim was not that Jesus had been restored to life (in the sense that the writer of the Fourth Gospel tells us that Lazarus was restored to life, the meaning of which is perfectly plain and evidence for which might in principle be forthcoming) but that he had been exalted into heaven. Furthermore he had been exalted into heaven *by God* in order to be with God; he had not resurrected himself. Thus the disciples' belief in the resurrection of Jesus and their confession of the risen Lord involved for the early Christians something far more fundamental and embracing than anything which could be confined to past event or present experience. It involved an interpretation of the history of Jesus in terms of the religious symbolism of apocalyptic, of resurrection of the dead, final judgement and the establishment of the kingdom of God. The new life of Jesus represented the first-fruits of the life of the new age, the beginning of the End, when God would reign in glory.

These symbolic categories, then, acquire a double importance. First, without them we cannot understand what the early Christians signified by their affirmation that God had raised Jesus from the dead. Second, we cannot discuss the truth of their affirmation unless we also discuss the validity of this symbolism. Appeal neither to the evidence of the empty tomb nor to the evidence of the *post mortem* appearances of Jesus, nor both together, provides an adequate substitute, even if they are to be taken at their face value. When it is further remembered that it is debatable whether they ought to be taken at their face value—the story of the empty tomb may be untrustworthy, while the appearances may have been the consequence rather than the cause of the resurrection belief—the importance of the symbolic and interpretative structure, and of its application of Jesus, becomes still more obvious. But it is precisely this symbolic structure which we find strange today. Can we transpose it into a different idiom?

Jesus lived and died in the faith that the way he went was the expression of an obedient response to the calling of God. It was the way for man because it was also the way of God. It was preparation for, and anticipation of, God's kingdom. So he believed and so he taught. But Jesus was crucified and the kingdom had not come. To his disciples his death must have seemed the very contradiction of his faith. However noble his chosen way of sacrificial love, it could not conceivably have been the way appointed by God. God would not have allowed his Christ to be put to death on a cross. That, as Paul was later to point out,[8] was judged by the Law to be a proof of godlessness. Hence, Jesus' death signified his rejection by God. Death and destruction had once again triumphed over life and love. God was as distant and as silent as ever.

Then, with the suddenness and unexpectedness of miracle and revelation, the frame was broken and the picture changed. The causes of this change we cannot now for certain know. An empty tomb? A series of visionary experiences? A flash of insight and a transformed theological judgement? Whatever may have sparked off the change, the new picture is very different from the old. What formerly spoke of the absence of God now speaks of his presence. The death of Jesus is now seen not only as the culmination and completion of his own chosen way of life—it did not take much imagination to understand that, his life being what it was and the circumstances being what they were, his death followed with a certain tragic inevitability—but also as the expression and embodiment of the divine love. From the cross itself flow springs of living water. It is the instrument of divine judgement and mercy, the means of forgiveness and reconciliation. Jesus is the minister of divine healing in death as in life. Death itself, the last enemy, has been compelled into the service of life. Jesus died. But that is no longer the end of his story. He continues to make the Holy and Gracious One present to men. Therefore he lives, in and with the life of God and in the lives of his followers. He lives and is the Lord.

Thus his followers proclaimed that Jesus had indeed been the Christ, that his teaching, life and death were effective symbols of the divine presence, and that he still possessed the power to communicate the grace and love of God. The ambiguities of secular existence had not been suddenly resolved. Nor had men been transported into a different and heavenly world. Death and the threat of the void still remained. But with the new structuring of perception and shaping of response they had been deprived of their ultimacy and robbed of their terror. Faith and hope in God had been renewed. 'Blessed be the God and Father of our Lord Jesus Christ! By his great mercy we have been born anew to a living hope through the resurrection of Jesus Christ from the dead.'[9]

Is a belief in the resurrection of Jesus Christ from the dead still a live option for us today? I suggest that it is, not least in the way and in the terms that I have just been outlining. But let me try to be honest about what has been going on.

First, I have of intention spoken elusively when I have used the expression 'Jesus lives'. I have not attempted to say with any degree of precision how this phrase is to be fully understood. Rather, I have linked it closely with the livingness of God, and have suggested that the risen life of Jesus is at least in part to be understood in terms of the continuing power of his words and deeds and sufferings, that is, of his person, to communicate to men a faith in the abiding graciousness and trustworthiness of God. It is not that by remembering him men give life to Jesus; it is rather that by remembering him they are given life by God. Jesus has a risen life because God communicates his own life through him. He lives in the present because God lives in the present. He is the same yesterday, today and for ever. He continues to mediate God to men. And, if this is in fact the case, it is perhaps not a downright misuse of words to say that he 'lives', or that 'God raised him from the dead'. No doubt more ought to be said. At least this much, I suggest, may and must be said.

Second, I have loosened the links which have traditionally been made between belief in the resurrection of Jesus and the traditions of the empty tomb and the *post mortem* appearances. I have not gone so far as to deny the truth of these traditions, but I have suggested that their truth is not necessarily an essential part of the meaning of the belief or an essential condition of its validity. Hence acceptance of the affirmation that God raised Jesus from the dead may be grounded on other considerations. These other considerations are complex; but, in brief, they may be taken to include, on the one hand, the recognition of an ultimate dimension within the structures of man's secular existence, this ultimate presenting itself as ambivalent and ambiguous, as promise or threat, as fullness or void; and on the other hand, as the apprehension, mediated through Jesus, and partly intuitive and partly reflective, since it takes the form both of new perspective and of new judgement, that this ultimate is in fact holy and good, gracious and trustworthy. In this sense and in this way it is still possible for men to come to experience Jesus as the Christ of God. The pieces of the jig-saw take on a new pattern.

So far we have been spelling out the implications of resurrection faith in terms of the ultimacy of the way of Jesus in response to the graciousness and trustworthiness of God. The way of Jesus *is* the way of Life. Whatever indications may appear to the contrary, however strongly men may feel themselves forced to find their happiness and fulfilment in the protection and pursuit of their own interests within the sphere of conflicting claims and counter-claims, the way of sacrificial love expresses the divine–human order. Such a faith stresses the eternal presence of God *despite* his apparent absence from the world.

However, the original resurrection faith also included a hope *for* the world. In the apocalyptic symbolism the resurrection of the dead was to be succeeded by a final judgement and the recreation of heaven and earth. The kingdom of God would come in power. How, then, are we to understand today this future kingdom of God for which Jesus hoped and prayed, and for which Christians, proclaiming the risen Christ, continue to hope and pray in Jesus' own words? In our own interpretation and appropriation of the apocalyptic imagery is this central symbol to be moved to the periphery or even forgotten? Has it not an essential logical function to perform even in the symbolic language of apocalyptic? Does it not provide the final verification of the faith that Jesus has been raised from the dead and lives in glory? And in the idiom which we ourselves have outlined, in which belief in the resurrection of Jesus is not to be verified so much by appeals to the empty tomb or the *post mortem* appearances as by the new perspective and the new judgement, is there not an even greater need for future verification of this faith? In what sense is *God* ultimately trustworthy if his *world* continues indefinitely to speak as much of his absence as of his presence? Is the Good News a basis for faith (of a sort), but not for hope?

Some interpreters have argued that the symbol of the coming kingdom of God should be divested of its temporal, historical and worldly connotations, and that it should be referred to an utterly distinct sphere, the non-temporal relation of the individual to God. In this way hope of the coming kingdom is closely assimilated to faith in the living Christ. The symbol of the kingdom is scarcely to be distinguished from the symbol of the resurrection. Respond to the proclamation of the gospel, it might be said, allow yourself to be challenged by its demand and recreated by its grace, and you will be risen with Christ and a citizen of the kingdom of God. The kingdom of God came and comes with Jesus Christ. He was and is the kingdom. And the kingdom comes again and again whenever individual men and women respond to his gospel, are set free from their worldly existence and self-understanding and offer an unworldly obedience to God. Thus in his Gifford Lectures Rudolf Bultmann declared:

> According to the New Testament, *Jesus Christ is the eschatological event*, the action of God by which God has set an end to the old world. In the preaching of the Christian Church the eschatological event will ever again become present and does become present ever and again in faith. The old world has reached its end for the believer, he is 'a new creature in Christ'. For the old world has reached its end with the fact that he himself as 'the old

man' has reached his end and is now 'a new man', a free man.[10]

And Bultmann goes on to quote with approval some words of Erich Frank:

> In his faith the Christian is a contemporary of Christ, and time and the world's history are overcome. The advent of Christ is an event in the realm of eternity which is incommensurable with historical time. But it is the trial of the Christian that although in the spirit he is above time and the world, in the flesh he remains in this world, subject to time; and the evils of history, in which he is engulfed, go on.[11]

So history and the world are swallowed up in the kingdom of God, for in that kingdom they have no place. In eternity the 'time' of grace and the 'time' of glory coincide.

Other interpreters have taken the future-directedness of the hope of the kingdom with the utmost seriousness, but have secularised the apocalyptic imagery. They have traced the progress of the kingdom in the past and have extrapolated it into the future, thereby nourishing a hope of a glory that will surely come. They have put their trust in Evolution, or Progress, or the Dialectic of History. God is working his purpose out in the affairs of men, and the time is drawing near when the earth 'shall be filled with the glory of God, as the waters cover the sea'. Future hope is retained. Nevertheless, secularised apocalyptic substitutes dubious gods for the Lord of heaven and earth, and the apocalyptic theme of the sudden and unexpected coming of his kingdom in judgement as well as in fulfilment is quietly forgotten. Furthermore, in the short run the secular future remains distinctly ambiguous; while in the long run it is hard to deny that man's world will one day come to an end, even if in the meantime he discovers resources of wisdom and selflessness sufficient to restrain him from bringing an untimely end upon himself.

We seem to be on the horns of a dilemma. If we wish to preserve the absolute goodness and holiness of God and the ultimacy of life lived in obedience and faith, we may quickly find ourselves setting eternity over against time and man's existence in relation to God over against his existence in the world. Time and history are essentially godless, and eternal life is to be discovered only in a series of timeless and intrinsically unrelated presents. This, however, represents a radical departure from our secular understanding of the nature of man, whose existence for good and ill is rooted in nature and history and shaped in the processes of becoming. It also represents a radical departure from the biblical understanding of God, man and the world. For God is the Lord of nature and of history, the Creator as well as the Redeemer; man is an ensouled body, not a pure spirit incarcerated in flesh. The world is the object of God's care and delight rather than the source of sin and evil. On the other hand, if we begin with man's temporal existence in worldly history, and emphasise that God does not save man by reconstituting him into a being for whom time and history are no longer significant, but gives him a new hope for the future, then the future itself, open though it may be, does not appear to be open enough to suggest a promise and blessing of fulfilment. From dust man came, and to dust he will return—and his world with him. Thus, either eternity swallows up time, or time swallows up eternity. In both cases, though in different ways, we face the end of man. What, then, is the meaning of his faith and hope in God?

The only way to escape from this dilemma, if we wish to

maintain both faith and hope, would seem to be in an attempt to re-think our concept of time and eternity in such a way that they are no longer mutually contradictory. If it is possible to think of God's eternity as inclusive of man's time, and of man's time as being taken up and fulfilled in God's eternity, then we may be able to retain both faith and hope. If, for example, the resurrection of Jesus from the dead can be given a richer content than that which we gave it earlier; that is, if 'Jesus lives' means not simply that his life, teaching and death continue to focus and mediate to man the *life of God*, but also that *he himself* now lives in God, in continuity with his earthly life, although in a discontinuity of mode of life, then we can perhaps talk of the fulfilment of time in eternity and the fulfilment of history in the kingdom of God. Of course, to talk in this way, granted that it even makes any sort of sense, is to talk speculatively. But perhaps we ought on occasions to speculate. As John Macquarrie has argued:

> It would seem that if we live with real hope for the world and if we are to work for its future with some confidence that what we are doing is worthwhile, we are committed to some kind of speculative eschatology . . . Hope, after all, would not be hope if it were based on infallible calculation. Neither should it be confused with optimism. Hope, like faith, is a risk that we take as finite existents, and perhaps we can hardly help taking it.[12]

Thus the believer may distinguish between the ultimate and the penultimate, between the future of God and the future of the world. His ultimate hope is directed towards the kingdom of God, beyond death and beyond the structures of the world. This ultimate hope is nourished by his belief that God has raised Jesus from the dead into his kingdom beyond death. At the same time his penultimate hope is for a 'better world' here and now, that is, for a world in which the creative and redemptive love of God is more fully realised. This penultimate hope is nourished both by his ultimate hope and also by those features of his secular experience which support and encourage an affirmative attitude towards the future, and which he reads as signs of the providence of God in nature, history and the lives of individual men and women.

> Belief in the resurrection and the kingdom is grounds for believing in openness, alterability and possibility, and through this, is grounds for hope. *Experience* of openness, alterability and possibility provides grounds for hope. *Somehow* they corroborate each other, reinforce each other, inform each other, while maintaining independence of each other.[13]

The idea of an ultimate hope which embraces a resurrection of the dead into a re-created world, discontinuous with but fulfilling life in the world as we know it, is a very fragile idea. Is it conceivable? Would not the very discontinuity envisaged entail that it could in no proper sense be called a *fulfilment* of life in this world? If so, not even omnipotence could bring it to pass. Is it desirable? Is not *human* joy so interwoven with caring, striving, achievement, failure, alteration and succession that the joys of the kingdom of God would not be human joys at all? It is notoriously difficult to give a satisfying imaginative substance to life in heaven. It is difficult, but perhaps not altogether impossible.

> And into that gate they shall enter, and in that house they shall dwell, where there shall be no Cloud nor Sun, no darknesse nor dazling, but one equall light, no noyse nor

silence, but one equall musick, no fears nor hopes, but one equall possession, no foes nor friends, but one equall communion and Identity, no ends nor beginnings; but one equall eternity.[14]

Nevertheless, the suspicion remains that it is better to travel hopefully than to arrive, and that the function of hope is to give immediate direction to the journeying rather than to promise an ultimate journey's end. It is, then, not surprising that those who have wished to retain some form of an ultimate hope in God have suggested that, although man and his world may well perish as individual men and women perish, yet they may hope to contribute to the life of God and obtain an 'objective' immortality in his memory. With God nothing of value is lost. He does not forget. Might it, however, be that with God to re-member is to re-create?

7

PRESENCE AND PROMISE

Beloved, we are God's children now; it does not yet
appear what we shall be, but we know that when he
appears we shall be like him. (1 John 3.2)

Is the hope of glory blessing or bane? Is it an enduring theological reality or a fleeting psychological illusion? The ear-
liest Christians, it would appear, believed that they were
living in the last days, between the old age and the new, and
looked for the coming of God's promised kingdom of
righteousness and peace. But they were disappointed. The
kingdom did not come. It was, in Dom Aelred Graham's
striking phrase, 'the great non-event'. 'The aspiration of the
Lord's Prayer', he writes, '"Thy kingdom come," remains
unfulfilled. The Messianic kingdom, as it was understood
by Jesus' contemporaries to have been announced by him,
never came. This is the great "non-event".'[1] It is not surprising, then, that he speaks of eschatology, the doctrine of the
last things, as 'the aspect of the Christian proclamation
around which there is the largest question mark'.[2]

However, eschatology cannot simply be dropped from
the Christian proclamation. It is no mere prediction of the
end of the world, attached like some appendix to the main

and otherwise self-sufficient text of Christian teaching. It affects our judgements concerning the significance of the slowly evolving processes of nature and of the course of human history. It affects our concepts of time and eternity. Above all it affects our understanding of God himself and of his relation as Creator to his creation. For it embodies the notion of a divine promise, such that God's faithfulness to his promise grounds man's endurance and sustains his hope even when the heavens themselves seem to be collapsing around his head. Call and promise are part of one and the same divine-human covenant. 'He who calls you is faithful and he will do it.'[3] Yes, indeed. But do what?

As we have already seen, there have not been lacking those who have wished to discount the beliefs of the early Christians, mistaken as they have turned out to be, and to interpret the imagery of God's coming kingdom in ways which harmonise with their experience. Some have simply revised the original chronology, and have prophesied another and still future time when God's kingdom would come. These times have been many and various, but they have all suffered the same fate. They have come and gone, but the world has continued as before. Others, still hopeful, but less sanguine, have postponed the kingdom's coming into the indefinite future, thus preserving the letter but not the substance of the early hope. For the more indefinite the future hope is, the less it is able to inspire confidence and courage in the present. (Doubtless I can be deeply concerned with, and influenced by, what is going to happen in my own life-time, or even what is going to happen in the life-time of my children. But what of the life-time of my grandchildren's grandchildren, and distant generations beyond? Are there not limits to my imagination and even to my whole-hearted concern?) Others, again, have abandoned all idea of a coming of God's kingdom in this world of space and time, and have transferred the imagery to another world, one which awaits each individual at his death. Yet others have redirected attention from the future to the past. The kingdom of God has already come, in the life, death and resurrection of Jesus.

This last interpretation, that Jesus himself was and is the kingdom of God, strained through it undoubtedly is, embodies, I suggest, an important, indeed fundamental, insight; namely, that the way of Jesus is also the way of God. God's rule is the rule of sacrificial love. In Jesus the divine love finds human expression. The Word is made flesh. Nevertheless, we can hardly refrain from asking: is the way of the kingdom also the fullness of kingdom itself? Is there no consummation of love to be anticipated? Does the kingdom remain for all time hidden? Has the new age finally *and fully* arrived? If we keep in mind the *hopes* engendered by the imagery of God's kingdom, it is difficult not to concede some validity to John Macquarrie's piquant comment: 'If eschatology has been realized, well, it is rather a damp squib.'[4]

It is the merit of Bultmann's reinterpretation of eschatological imagery in terms of an existential theology that, by referring it to the moment of decision, he rescues it from the unreality of an indefinite and incredible future, makes it immediately relevant to the lives of individual men and women in any and every age, and recovers the sense of urgency and ultimacy which the imagery possessed in its original context. As Bultmann depicts human existence, every man lives his life in the movement of time from the past through the present and into the future. In every present he may be confronted with a fundamental choice between two opposed understandings of himself. Either he can approach the future on the assured basis of his past; or he can open himself to make a radical response to the call of the future. If he chooses the former, he becomes a slave of his past—in the language of Paul, he seeks to justify himself by works. If he chooses the latter, he can be set free from the past and receive the gift of himself from the future—in the language of Paul, he can be saved by grace through faith. This freedom from the past cannot be his own achievement or possession. It can come to him only from beyond himself. The call and the gift occur in the proclamation of Jesus Christ. Thus 'Jesus Christ is the eschatological event not as an established fact of past time but as repeatedly present, as addressing you and me here and now in preaching.'[5] And he ends his Gifford lectures with the celebrated peroration, itself almost an act of preaching:

> Man who complains: 'I cannot see meaning in history, and therefore my life, interwoven in history, is meaning-less', is to be admonished: do not look around yourself into universal history, you must look into your own per-sonal history. Always in your present lies the meaning in history, and you cannot see it as a spectator, but only in your responsible decisions. In every moment slumbers the possibility of being the eschatological moment. You must awaken it.[6]

Bultmann recovers, as I have said, the sense of urgency and ultimacy which belonged to the original imagery. Every moment contains the possibility of a choice between life and death, heaven and hell, salvation and damnation, the freedom of grace and the tyranny of sin. Nevertheless, this concentration of the eschatological imagery within the moment of decision, despite its initial appeal, involves some less appealing consequences. Existential time is cut off from historical time. The moment of decision, so far as its religious significance is concerned, stands alone. Nothing of religious importance is contributed to it by what precedes and leads up to it; for the past is precisely that which enslaves a man and from which he needs to be set free. Nothing of religious significance flows from it and follows after it; for if that were allowed to be the case, it might suggest that a man possessed at least some measure of power to co-operate in his own salvation. Furthermore, if the consequences which flowed from the decision into historical time themselves had some religious value, then, when time moved on and these consequences themselves belonged to the past, it might be expected that they too would have some positive contribution to make to any future decision.

Existential time cannot be separated from historical time, as Bultmann would have us believe. Man's life is not only interwoven 'in' history; it is also interwoven 'with' history. History provides not only the context for man's life in faith, but also forms part of it. Bultmann, on the other hand, seems to prize apart the *form* of openness, freedom and decision from its material *content* in the individual's own embodied history or in the universal history of man and the world. According to him, man makes his decisions *towards* the future—without 'futurity' there could be no decision—and God calls him to obedience *from* the future; but the future itself has little or nothing to contribute to life in God's kingdom. Once again, hope is swallowed up by faith. The imagery of the kingdom of God retains its original urgency, even, in Bultmann's sense, its ultimacy; for the decision of faith is the choice of 'life' rather than 'death'. But does it retain its fullness?

We find ourselves returning yet again to the question which has already tormented us, the question implicit in the description of the hoped-for coming of the kingdom of God as 'the great non-event'. Is eschatological hope a cheat? Is it a dream of what never was and never will be? Has the mythical Golden Age of the past, discredited by our knowledge of man's origins and history, simply been succeeded by an equally mythical Golden Age of the future? Is it only illusion, offering psychological compensation to those who suffer from an unbearable reality in the present? If the Catholic Dom Aelred Graham puts a question mark after the whole idea of eschatology, the Jewish Rabbi Richard Rubinstein puts a line right through it:

> 'Eschatology is a sickness'. . . . It was our Jewish sickness originally. We gave it to you [Christians]. You took us seriously. Would that you hadn't! . . . If you are a Christian, you cannot avoid it. If you become post-Christian, choose pagan hopelessness rather than the false illusion of apocalyptic life.[7]

Hope looks forward expectantly to the future. It draws its strength from that which is not yet but which may perhaps come to be; from the possible rather than the actual. Without the dimension of temporality it has no meaning. But it is precisely the dimension of temporality that renders hope suspect. For is not time the universal destroyer? And what time does not destroy, will not man himself destroy? Is it not a symptom of man's powerlessness that he dreams of a paradise which will reverse the pains and ambiguities of his actual world? And when man acquires power beyond his forebears' wildest dreams, is it not a symptom of his folly and blindness that he envisages a utopia which he himself will create through his own titanic efforts?

Man's life in the world demands thought and action, purpose and planning, striving and achievement or failure; in short, care for the morrow. But there are moments in human experience when care gives place to enjoyment, activity is unimpeded and fulfilling, time stops still and a sense of immediacy and totality supervenes. Such experiences are various and differ in their intensity. They have sometimes been used to provide analogues for the hoped-for life of heaven. For example, the language of sexual intercourse has provided an analogy for the rapturous union of the blessed with God. Or, again, the language of dance and play has been used to suggest a joy which is immediate, spontaneous and carefree. C. S. Lewis once wrote:

> I do think that while we are in this 'valley of tears', cursed with labour, hemmed round with necessities, tripped up with frustrations, doomed to perpetual plannings, puzzlings, and anxieties, certain qualities that must belong to the celestial condition have no chance to get through, can project no image of themselves, except in activities which, for us here and now, are frivolous. . . . It is only in our 'hours-off ', only in our moments of permitted festivity, that we find an analogy. Dance and game *are* frivolous, unimportant down here; for 'down here' is not their natural place. . . . That which, if it could be prolonged here, would be a truancy, is likest that which in a better country is the End of ends. Joy is the serious business of Heaven.[8]

If, however, there should be no heavenly city awaiting the faithful at the end of their earthly pilgrimage, ought we not to explore those experiences of 'heaven' which occur here and now? If God is absent, do not such experiences still provide the stuff of religion? If man no longer hopes in a future salvation, should he not seek present illumination? Was not Bultmann right in directing our attention to the present moment, but wrong in accentuating the decision of faith rather than the immediacy of experience?

There are certain experiences which do not simply colour and sweeten the rest of life, but in a striking way stand out from the rest of life and, as it were, turn it upside-down. Such experiences the psychologist, Abraham Maslow, has called 'peak-experiences'. He discusses them in considerable detail and describes their characteristics, of which the following are only a sample:

> It is quite characteristic in peak-experiences that the whole universe is perceived as an integrated and unified whole. . . . Perception in the peak-experiences can be relatively ego-transcending, self-forgetful, egoless, unselfish. It can come closer to being unmotivated, impersonal, desireless, detached, not needing or wishing. . . . The peak-experience is felt as a self-validating, self-justifying moment which carries its own intrinsic value with it. . . . Many people find this so great and high an experience that it justifies not only itself but even living itself. Peak-experiences can make life worthwhile by their occasional occurrence. . . . In the peak-experience there is a very characteristic disorientation in time and space, or even the lack of consciousness of time and space. . . . The world seen in the peak-experiences is seen only as beautiful, good, desirable, worthwhile, etc., and is never experienced as evil or undesirable. The world is accepted. . . . Evil itself is accepted and understood and seen in its proper place in the whole, as belonging there, as unavoidable, as necessary, and, therefore, as proper. . . . This is another way of becoming 'god-like'. . . . In peak-experiences, the dichotomies, polarities, and conflicts of life tend to be transcended or resolved. . . . The conception of heaven that emerges

from the peak-experiences is one which exists all the time all around us, always available to step into for a little while at least.[9]

Thus the characteristics of these peak-experiences differ sharply from the characteristics of more mundane experiences and in some respects contradict them. Peak-experiences are all-absorbing, infinitely satisfying, timeless and perfect. The elements of striving, longing for what is no longer or is not yet, good and evil, freedom and care, which mark the temporal world of change and chance, of process and becoming, are lacking. They take the individual right out of the world and introduce him to a private 'world' of his own. They offer an immediate escape, 'salvation' here and now.

As a psychologist Maslow inclines to treat these peak-experiences naturalistically. He is interested in their causes and effects. He suggests that it may be possible to induce them artificially by hypnosis or the use of drugs and that they could have a therapeutic and integrating role to play in an individual's own psychological development. However, he goes on to suggest that these experiences provide the common core of religion.[10] They 'may be the model of the religious revelation or the religious illumination or conversion'.[11] Furthermore, they may be 'embedded either in a theistic, supernatural context or in a non-theistic context'.[12] The implication seems to be that it is the experience itself, private and transitory though it is, that is of fundamental significance, and that the interpretations of the experience, which attempt to say something concerning that of which it is an experience, are secondary, if not mutually contradictory. They are symbolic projections, castles in the air constructed out of the same experiential bricks. The castles may rise and then collapse, but the bricks remain.

It is not surprising that many who find their mundane experience of life to be a kind of imprisonment should long for an experience which promises immediate release and cultivate it for its own sake. However, human existence remains, for at least a lifetime, a worldly existence; and the problem arises, both at practical and at theoretical levels, how the two divergent kinds of experience, peak and off-peak, are to be related. 'While the thirst for totality, for the infinite, is a basic and wonderful part of our makeup, it tends to claim more for itself than it can really achieve. Total unity is of the moment, and the other element of longing, the longing for the "more" of the future, is if anything more essential.'[13]

An older tradition of mysticism, while not despising these transitory experiences, though regarding them with some suspicion just in so far as they may distract and deter from a deeper and lasting illumination, has developed a way of intellectual and moral discipline by which an individual's consciousness may be thoroughly transformed and he may come to know that he is one with the ultimate, that the point of view of the empirical, time-bound, desiring and striving ego is a false point of view, and that his real self is one of pure consciousness, eternal and changeless, identical with the absolute Self. Salvation consists in realising this truth in the face of appearances, of losing one's partial and relative point of view in the complete and absolute point of view. From such a 'point of view' all is already perfect. It was only ignorance which imagined that it was anything but perfect.

Enlightenment, then, involves a totally different way of facing and intending the world from that in which a man looks towards the open future in hope or fear. As John Passmore puts the point:

Very often the mystic sets out to free himself from care by denying the existence of the future. Time, he suggests, is unreal, an illusion; in reality, there is only the present, the 'Everlasting Now'. There is no future for men to care about. If men fasten all their affection, the mystic tells us, upon that 'Everlasting Now'—given such names as God, the One, the Universe as a Whole—they will no longer have any need for care. It is the only object which men can love without giving hostages to fortune. They can unite with it without any fear that it will change, because it is immutable; there need be no fear that it contains secret threats which will only later be revealed, for it is absolutely simple; there is no risk that it, and through it those who love it, will suffer, for it is impassible. So man's relationship with the Everlasting Now can be unalloyed enjoyment, entirely carefree.'[14]

To some, the love of the Everlasting Now may seem to be the epitome of true religion. It releases man from the conflicts and ambiguities of the temporal world, for the ultimate One is that in which all conflicts and ambiguities are resolved. It also releases him from the desires and strivings of his empirical ego, for in the enjoyment of the Everlasting Now there is no place for striving and desire. Enlightened himself, he is now free to minister enlightenment to those who are imprisoned in their false consciousness.

That there is an attractiveness and strength in this interpretation of religion is undeniable. However, it is purchased at a price. It seems to have as a corollary the implication that the temporal world is somehow unreal, or illusory, and that the desires of men and women to shape a new and better world within the structures of space and time have no ultimate point or validity. Reality as interpreted in terms of the Everlasting Now seems to conflict with reality as interpreted in terms of time. Therefore they cannot both be equally real. Time must 'disappear' from the viewpoint of eternity. To ascribe value and reality to the desiring, striving, planning, creative ego, to the processes of becoming, to the openness of the future and the freedom of man, is questionable if not logically impossible. To say this is not to deny the fact that mystics have often also been men of action, for they have returned after their experience of enlightenment to the world of illusion in order to share their knowledge with suffering humanity. They have been moved by compassion. Nevertheless, their action, and even their compassion, seems bound to stem from, and may even reflect, a more fundamental non-involvement, necessitated by an understanding of eternity which renders time and history unreal and illusory.

Anxious to avoid these consequences, some philosophers of the mystical tradition[15] have argued that the temporal world is not to be rejected in this way. In 'the logic of the infinite' time and eternity are not contradictory and mutually exclusive characteristics. Hence the processes of becoming, in so far as they are understood to be working towards an eschatological fulfilment, are themselves to be understood as a perfect manifestation of an eternal perfection.

Is this a plausible solution of the apparent antinomy? Let us grant that it is conceivable that the ultimate One may have both eternal and temporal characteristics; that its eternity may include an everlastingness. Do not other, perhaps more intractable, contradictions still remain? For the temporal world is admittedly full of suffering, evil, frustration and imperfection. How, then, can this world be called a perfect manifestation of eternal perfection, even if it is to culminate in a perfect *eschaton*?

The following resolution of the dilemma is sometimes suggested. Evil, suffering, frustration and imperfection, it is said, are really what they seem to be, whether from the point of view of eternity or from a point of view within time. Nevertheless, from the viewpoint of eternity the temporal process, a process in which evil and imperfection occur but in which they are destined finally to be transformed and overcome, is *as a whole* the perfect manifestation of eternal perfection. Evil and imperfection are necessary constituents of temporal perfection. An analogy is sometimes drawn between such a way of viewing time and history and the way in which a particular blemish may contribute to the beauty of a whole painting, or a particular disharmony to the harmony of a whole piece of music.

The plausibility of this line of argument rests on the *identification* of the individual's viewpoint with that of the ultimate One. Through such identification evil may acquire an instrumental goodness, and *sub specie aeternitatis* I may see my suffering and that of others as the manifestation of goodness. I have no reason to protest against the goodness of the ultimate One on the grounds that *my* suffering is instrumental to *his* enjoyment, and that therefore I am being immorally used as a means to his end, since, rightly understood, his enjoyment *is* my enjoyment. The protest is misconceived.

But is such identification to be accepted? Or is this the point at which there opens up a fundamental difference between two types of religion, the mystical and the prophetic, since for the latter God remains other than man, standing over against him and addressing him, and man's identification with God remains for every state of consciousness the ultimate blasphemy? The mystical identification of man and God may contain within it the seeds of peace and joy.

But what of individual freedom, creativity and hope? What room is left for the intrinsic value and reality of the individual person in his own concrete particularity, as a focussed centre of responsible and responsive activity? Is man in his relation to the Ultimate as a wave to the Ocean, or as a son to his Father?

I have permitted myself something of a digression. Let me now return to my more immediate concern, which is the relation of present and future in the Christian understanding of God and his kingdom. We have been considering the claim that certain peak-experiences, or a certain enlightened state of consciousness, offer man salvation in the present through a reconstruction of his basic structures of perceiving and intending the world. We have suggested that such a reconstruction tends to the devaluation of the temporal and historical world, as well as of the responsible and responsive self. The idea of love itself, divine and human, undergoes a subtle but significant transformation. Let us now explore this latter idea a little further.

The mystic way tends to the total abnegation of the desires of the individual self in the one perfect joy of the absolute Self. Such self-abnegation is sometimes assumed to belong also to the way of sacrificial love which Jesus lived and proclaimed. But is this the case? However much we stress Jesus' teaching concerning the love of the Heavenly Father for his children, and the consequent impropriety of anxious self-concern, does not his equally emphatic teaching concerning the love of neighbour involve a persistent desire, care and concern, namely, for the neighbour's good? Desire is not to be eliminated, it is to be transformed and redirected, from oneself to one's neighbour. Furthermore, it is to be directed towards the neighbour in his concrete particularity. He is to be loved, not simply for God's sake, but also for his own sake. The love of neighbour is indeed the service of God; for the neighbour is also the object of God's creative and redemptive love. Yet the love of neighbour does not thereby become merely a means of serving God, for it is grounded in the neighbour's own needs as much as in the commandment of God. One might perhaps say that the love of neighbour is a reflection and expression of God's own love for that neighbour, so that it becomes imperative to love the neighbour for his own sake if he is at the same time to be loved for God's sake.

Human love, at its deepest and purest, has a double aspect, compounding both present and future. It rejoices in the present and cares for the future. 'A love devoid of enjoyment is not love at all, it is what Cudworth called "slavish imposition," duty masquerading as love. But a love devoid of care, equally, is simple enjoyment pretending to be love.'[16] As present experience love is complete, fulfilled, impervious to time and change. It is a moment of revelation, of meeting, of sheer joy. Lovers accept and delight in each other exactly as they are. But lovers who are not bemused by their love know that they too belong to the world of time and change. Therefore each cares that the other shall continue to exist, to grow and to flourish. While they may experience their love as eternal, at the same time they pledge each other to undying fidelity. If time offers a threat to love, such that each takes on himself responsibility for the other's future, and both together for their continuing love, love itself seems to offer a promise, that time will only renew and deepen love, not destroy it. Love engenders hope. 'To love a being is to say, "Thou shalt not die."'[17]

Love is not just a concern for another in the moment of encounter (as is often eloquently said today); it is also concern for the other's future. Love is 'walking along the way with him'. Thus, although in its more intense form, Christian existence means a disregard for one's future, this is correlated with a concern for another's future, which brings immediate practical hopes and long-range hopes into relevance.[18]

Hope, then, is not necessarily the child of want and impotence. It may also be the child of a present and anticipatory experience of the fullness of love. It is both the glory and the tragedy of human loves that they give rise to unlimited hope and yet recognise that in the end, sooner or later, this hope is to be frustrated by time and death. Human loves come to an end, even if their memory is stronger than death. What, however, occurs if and when we introduce God into the human story and acknowledge his presence as the source and sustainer of the deepest human love? Do time and death retain their ultimate power and significance? Or are they thereby reduced to the status of penultimates, limits which may themselves now be transcended?

Reflection on the nature of God and on his covenant-relation to Israel itself produced in the course of Israelite history the idea of a future kingdom and of a resurrection of the dead. Not even death could thwart his purposes of love. The idea of a resurrection was indeed hotly contested. It was barely conceivable. Accepted by the Pharisees, it was rejected by the Sadducees. The argument went both ways. The early Christians, however, proclaimed the theological possibility as a religious certainty. The barely conceivable was in fact conceivable because it had now become actual. God had raised *Jesus* from the dead. The doctrine had been realised in an individual person.

If we are to attempt to make any sense of this at all, we

must, as I have already suggested, concentrate our attention neither on the story of the empty tomb nor on the witness to the *post mortem* appearances of Jesus, whatever significance is properly to be given to these traditions in the structure of Christian proclamation as a whole. Rather, we must attend to the underlying logic of love, of which faith and hope, presence and promise, are mutually related aspects. It is the recognition and acknowledgement of the reality of the divine love which ground both faith and hope, assuring man that all is well and that all shall be well. It was this recognition and acknowledgement that constituted Jesus' own fundamental perspective and orientation, and it was the same recognition and acknowledgement which constituted the fundamental perspective and orientation of the early Church. However, the communication of this faith and hope in the divine love from Jesus to his disciples was no simple or continuous process. It was marked by a radical discontinuity, the death of Jesus on the cross, and the apparent contradiction of the substance of his proclamation and life. It seemed all too obvious that he had spoken and lived an illusion, not the truth, and that God was not the heavenly Father, creator and ruler, whom he had affirmed him to be. Evil and death had turned out to be stronger than goodness and life.

Then came the miracle. The story of Jesus had not ended. The conviction of the presence of divine love which had been his, and which he had attempted, with only limited success, to communicate to his disciples during his life, was somehow or other renewed in them after his death. Now they understood more fully, for their own fundamental perspective and orientation had undergone a decisive change. The death of Jesus had not invalidated this perspective and orientation. It had been instrumental in its communication.

The way of Jesus had not been based on an illusion of God, but on the truth of God. He continued to mediate the presence and love of God to his disciples. His hope in God had not been utterly disappointed. It had been fulfilled in an unexpected, strange, but totally congruous, way. The discontinuity of death itself had been subsumed into a continuity of Jesus' God-communicating love. Jesus lived.

The early Christians' experience and conviction of the divine love's continuing to reach out to them through Jesus itself embodied the double aspect of love, of presence and promise. They experienced a new order of things. They were like men who themselves had died and been raised from the dead, or who had undergone a new birth. The present love of God gave them a new joy, and it was as if they were already living in a new age, impervious to time and change. They were in the present of the lovers' moment of encounter. And this present love itself engendered a new hope; for despite the immediacy and 'timelessness' of their lovers' meeting with God in the present, they were still creatures of time and history, subject to the vicissitudes of change and chance. What, then, might they hope for? They could not know. If they had not been able to foresee the triumph of the divine love over death, in that God had raised Jesus from the dead, how could they foresee what future triumphs of the same love might come to pass. But their hope, which was grounded in the divine love, did not need to spell out the contents of that for which they hoped. In principle, nothing was beyond the bounds of their hope. If the kingdom of God's love could embrace and annul the negativity of death, might it not also in the end embrace and annul the negativities of time and history? If the life of the man Jesus was fulfilled in and through death, might not the life of mankind, even of the world, be fulfilled in some analogous way?

Whatever the future might hold in store, they were confident of one thing at least, namely, that it would embody and express the same love as had been embodied and expressed in Jesus. Hence in God's future *Jesus* would come again and again. And in the final, hoped-for coming, *his* would be the last judgement and eternal life.

Christian prayer for the coming of God's kingdom draws its strength from an acknowledgement of the presence, and hence an expectation of the futurity, of God's absolute love. Love shapes its own special combination of faith and hope, of mysticism and eschatology. Time becomes the sacrament and effective symbol of eternity. The limits of our finite world, including its sufferings and losses, become the conditions, and even the instruments, of Love's creative and redemptive work. And if they are the conditions and instruments, will they also be the final frustration and defeat of him who wills to love his creatures into being? Or when the divine love finds its fulfilment in the perfect response of a human love, have these conditions and limits no further function to perform, and will they be allowed to pass away?

The secret of the world of relationships and persons is not found by those who seek to escape from the world of objects and of things, but it is open to all who allow the latter world in all the width of its manifold variety to become to them the medium for the revelation of the former in all the depth of its unfathomable intensity. Thus we live by faith in a world which love transforms, and we live in hope of a world which love will have transformed.[19]

8

EXPERIMENT WITH LIFE

How long will you go limping with two different opinions? If the Lord is God, follow him. (1 Kgs 18.21)

In exploring the significance for human hope of the Christian symbol of the kingdom of God, and in extending our speculations beyond time into eternity, we may appear to have thrown caution to the winds and to have ridden roughshod over the half-believer's sensitivities and hesitations. To him we now return.

The half-believer would be the first to admit that he is open to the charge of limping with two different opinions. In the contest between those who believe and those who disbelieve in God he finds his own ground shifting. Now one side of the argument, now the other side gains the upper hand. He is conscious of the relative strengths and weaknesses of both positions. There are features of the worlds of nature and history which seem to him to count in favour of belief. There are other features which seem to him equally to count against belief. There is no single, simple scale on which the balance of opposing arguments can be definitively assessed. At times it might even appear that each side weighs all the arguments in its own scale, and that the two scales have nothing in common. Even if this is not the case, and room for rational debate remains, it has nevertheless to be admitted that the weight of evidence can vary according both to the total context in which it is placed and to the judgement of the one who does the weighing, a judgement which cannot be reduced to rule and calculation. Now context on the one hand, and judgement on the other, vary not only from individual to individual, or from group to group, but also from time to time within the individual himself. As his experience changes so also may his judgement and the context in which he makes the judgement.

The half-believer is a man in two minds. Were he not so obviously sane, he might be labelled schizophrenic. He cannot leave the question about God alone, but at the same time he is unable to give it an intellectually satisfying answer. Only God, it seemed, was in a position to know beyond a shadow of doubt that he existed; that is, if indeed he did exist. Arguments for his existence were inconclusive. Appeals to revelation were likewise inconclusive. The experience of those who professed to have an immediate awareness of God was open to more than one interpretation. And as for his own experience, such as it was, it could only be called ambiguous and fleeting. Thus there was no fixed starting-point from which the rest might more or less automatically follow. Rather, there were different ways of perceiving and understanding the world as a whole, each of which consisted of a vast number of interrelated and mutually supporting features, but none of which established an interpretative pattern which was unquestionably more simple, more coherent and more adequate than any of its rivals. Thus there was room for intellectual doubt. In fact doubt presented itself as an intellectual necessity. Furthermore, one might go so far as to say that, if reasoning and reflection were to be accorded their rightful place in human life, doubt was a kind of duty; at least to the extent that in the case of any total and all-embracing world-view that he might espouse the believer ought to admit that, in holding this view, he might very well be mistaken.

The half-believer is unable, once and for all, to make up his mind. He remains uncertain. But cannot his uncertainty, in one way or another, be side-stepped and disarmed?

It might, for example, be argued in the face of his uncertainty that there are numerous instances of belief outside the mathematical sciences in which a man has the right to be certain of the truth of a belief, even though there is always a logical possibility that he may be mistaken and his belief false. Such an argument is, of course, in itself valid. But it is beside the point. The logical possibility of my being mistaken infects almost all my beliefs. It is, indeed, such a logical possibility which has been the chief weapon in the armoury of radical scepticism. However, we have no need to be frightened of this particular bogey. The requirement that our beliefs should be reasonable, based on good evidence and supported by sound argument, is to be distinguished from the requirement that they should be logically necessary. The criteria of reasonable belief do not include that of logical necessity. On the other hand, it is by the criteria of reasonable belief that alternative world-views are to be assessed; and it is in the exercise of these criteria that doubt enters the door and establishes itself in the half-believer's living-room. His uncertainty remains.

Or, again, it might be argued that the fact that there are, objectively speaking, reasonable grounds for doubting a belief is no insuperable obstacle to my being certain about my belief. A distinction is to be drawn between an intellectual certainty and psychological certitude. However, the

129

application of this distinction to resolve the half-believer's uncertainty is itself a very uncertain procedure.

My feeling certain of the truth of a belief may perhaps stem from my having reasons for believing, even though these reasons are not transparently clear to me and I find it very difficult to articulate them coherently. In this case, I think, I may legitimately claim that my feeling of certainty is reasonably grounded, even though its reasonableness is not something that I can immediately establish either to my own or to others' satisfaction. Thus it is possible, if anyone so wishes, for him to speak in cases such as this of reasons of the heart of which the intellect is ignorant. It must, however, at the same time be insisted that, if the heart is in this way to be allowed its reasons, they must in principle, if they are to be reasons rather than aberrations, be such as will turn out on further reflection to be the kinds of consideration which the intellect can recognise as members of its own family.

My feeling of certainty may, on the other hand, have nothing to do with reason at all. It may be totally irrational. Or it may be based on 'reasons' which, on further reflection, I recognise to be no reasons at all. If in such circumstances I reject the appeal to reason in any shape or form, but continue to pride myself on my feeling so certain, and ascribe my certainty to an invincible faith, I have thereby abandoned all claims to rationality. Of course there is nothing to prevent my clinging to my irrational faith if I so decide. Decisions, as well as beliefs, can be irrational. I may even go so far as to exhort others to adopt a similar faith. But I cannot with any consistency argue with them that they ought to adopt such faith, for in so arguing I should be appealing to the same kind of reasoning as that which I had originally rejected. In short, unless one is prepared to countenance a sharp dichotomy between the intellect and the heart, the recognition of the presence and persistence of intellectual doubt must affect, and at the very least diminish, the full force of psychological certitude.

The half-believer lacks a feeling of certainty. His half-belief is such as to place such feeling beyond his grasp. He remains uncertain in his own mind what to believe; uncertain also what he himself in his heart of hearts really does believe. Were this uncertainty concerned only with a matter of theoretical and speculative interest, he could recognise and accept his divided mind without more ado. For all practical purposes he could ignore it. There would be no need for him to determine the issue one way or another. He could suspend judgement.

However, he does not see the matter in this light. Belief in God is not a theoretical and speculative affair concerning the distant powers which may or may not administer the universe. It is a matter of profoundly practical importance, since it concerns the way in which he is to perceive and intend his world, the manner in which he is to live his life and the sort of person he hopes to become. This in turn will affect his relationships with others and their relationships with him, and so contribute to the shaping of the human world which he and they will together inhabit. He cannot, then, escape the responsibility of decision. To suspend judgement will itself be one form of decision, with its own practical consequences. He has come to a fork in the road. Since he cannot stop and stay where he is, he must make up his mind which turning to take. He has to act according to the best light; and even if that light is half-darkness, nevertheless he still has to act. He must commit himself to one belief or the other.

We must, however, be careful when we speak of his committing himself to a belief. It may otherwise suggest that he resolves his intellectual uncertainty by an act of will. But this is not the case. If we pursue our analogy of the fork in the road, we shall say that he commits himself to a belief in so far as he decides which turning to take on the basis of reflection on which turning seems to him to hold out the greater promise of taking him further along his journey. He decides which way to go, thus resolving the uncertainty of practical indecision. In this sense, he has made up his mind. But in another sense, he may not have 'made up his mind'; for the arguments in favour of going this way or that are not suddenly changed by his decision, and may continue to be more or less evenly balanced. Intellectual uncertainty persists.

Deciding to believe, in the sense of deciding to act on the basis of a belief, is one thing; deciding to believe, in the sense of deciding to assent to a belief *ex animo*, is another. In the latter case believing, or disbelieving, is something which lies outside the sole jurisdiction of the will. It is to be determined by the weight of evidence, not by an act of will. It is not in dispute that, after weighing up the pros and cons of a belief, a man may judge that it is more likely to be true than false, or false than true. His judgement may then not inappropriately be called a decision; for after a period of indecision he comes down on one side of the fence rather than on the other. He decides, let us say, *that* the belief is probably true. But his decision does not make the belief true. Nor does he decide, as a way of resolving the conflicting arguments, *to* believe. For belief follows upon judgement, and judgement upon reflection and argument. The will is the servant of the intellect, not its master. There is something incongruous and suspect in all talk of the *will to believe*. A similar incongruity may, if we are not on our guard, infect our talk of commitment to a belief.

To sum up, the idea of committing oneself to a belief is ambiguous. There are many situations which call for action even when we are uncertain of the true nature of such situations. Action, and therefore commitment, is imperative. But commitment to action does not of itself render a belief any more or less certain. The consequences of action may provide further evidence which tends to confirm or invalidate the belief, or they may not. If the latter turns out to be the case, the uncertainty remains as it was before the action. Now one can act decisively on the basis of a belief that is only probable. One can even act decisively on the basis of a belief that is improbable, or downright unreasonable. However, the decisiveness of the action is one thing; the rational status of the belief is another. It is within my prerogative to determine to act decisively, it is not within my prerogative to determine to believe unreservedly. Thus it is important that we should be alert to the ambiguity latent in the idea of commitment to a belief. If it suggests commitment to action on the assumption that the belief, uncertain in itself, may nevertheless be true, there is nothing in the idea to arouse misgiving. Such commitment to belief is an everyday occurrence. We could not even survive for long, let alone achieve anything worthwhile, were it not. If, on the other hand, it is taken to suggest the resolution of doubt concerning the truth of a belief by some 'act of faith' which disposes once and for all of the question of truth and falsehood, then commitment to belief is a most improper business.

Commitment to belief in God offers no exception. So long as there are reasonably strong grounds for denying the existence of God, grounds recognised by believer and unbeliever alike, doubt must in principle remain the correlate of belief. To say this is not to say that all believers will necessarily also be doubters. The facts themselves show that this is not the case. There are believers who have no doubts. Nor is it to say that all believers ought also to be doubters. (Doubts may not occur to the believer because he is unaware of the intellectual difficulties inherent in his belief. Doubts simply have not arisen; and there is no overriding obligation on us to confront the believer with those intellectual difficulties which give rise to doubt. In certain circumstances an obligation of this kind may possibly exist, but it is hardly a universal and unexceptionable obligation.) It is, however, to suggest that, once the intellectual difficulties inherent in his belief have been fully drawn to his attention, especially in a culture in which alternative if equally problematic beliefs are widely held by persons whose integrity, insight and understanding he respects, the believer must accept the inevitability of doubt within himself. However compelling his own experience of God may seem to him, it is not self-authenticating, though it may in fact be veridical. However reasonable his belief may seem to him—and it may in fact be a true belief—the undeniable fact that it does not seem reasonable to others who have as good a claim as he has to be reckoned as reasonable human beings, should cause him at least a moment's hesitation. 'I beseech you, in the bowels of Christ, think it possible you may be mistaken.'[1] All attempts to ignore or to suppress such doubt are an offence against integrity.

Believers who reject the appeal of the irrational, who require that their belief in God shall be a reasonable belief, who also believe that they have good reasons for their belief, must nevertheless acknowledge the inevitability, perhaps also the propriety, of persistent intellectual doubt. However, the Christian proclamation not only affirms a set of beliefs, it also summons to a way of life. The 'doctrine' articulates, specifies and grounds the 'commitment'. At the centre of this commitment is a commitment to the way of sacrificial love, paradigmatically pictured in the teaching of Jesus and exemplified in his life and death. Thus the summons to the way of love ('Follow me') may continue to be clearly heard, even when the accompanying doctrine ('Who art thou, Lord?') proves difficult to believe. There is room for decision, either to walk the way of love or not. But what is involved in walking this way? Wherein lies its moral appeal?

It can be argued, not unconvincingly, that the way of love is in part justified by its fruits. It builds up, rather than tears down. It creates the kind of human life and relationships which we all recognise in our heart of hearts to be desirable. It can also be argued that it is the precondition of a responsive and responsible humanity. We are loved into becoming human by those who love us and continue to love us, not because of any merits we possess or because of our deserts, but because their love rejoices in our existence and desires our fulfilment. Such love 'is patient . . . kind and envies no one . . . is never boastful, nor conceited, nor rude; never selfish, not quick to take offence . . . keeps no score of wrongs; does not gloat over other men's sins, but delights in the truth'.[2] Such love, it may be argued, corresponds with the law of man's own nature. Nevertheless, it can hardly be called 'natural' without qualification. It may exercise a strong and reasonable claim upon our devotion; it may be apprehended as a proper human ideal. But it also stands over against us in judgement, calling in question our all-too-human limitations and the all-too-natural persuit of our own interests, regardless of those of others. Enlightened self-interest, for some the essence of rationality in practical affairs, may persuade us to restrain our own immediate interests and have regard to the interests of others. But neighbour-love cannot

135

be equated with enlightened self-interest. It exceeds it in its range of concern. It springs from the recognition of another's needs rather than from a calculated consideration of one's own. Self is forgotten in the moment of another's need.

We may say, then, that a decision to follow the way of love which Jesus exemplified is neither purely reasonable nor purely unreasonable. In part it converges with what a man may reasonably conceive to be the claims of humanity; in part it transcends it altogether. On those who recognise its appeal and power it exercises an authority which is both continuous and discontinuous with the promptings of their natural selves. It presents a vision and hope of a transfigured human nature, and at the same time a new criterion of reasonableness.

It has sometimes been suggested that to follow the way of sacrificial love *is* to believe in God. For such love is self-abnegation, the denial of one's own self-centred interests. Hence it cannot properly be called one's own love. Furthermore, such love is eternal; for it is unaffected by the contingencies of the world and the way in which things happen to go. Such love is therefore 'the Spirit of God, and to possess it is to walk with God'.[3] He who loves in this way, then, is properly said to know God. For 'to know God is to love Him. There is no theoretical understanding of the reality of God.'[4]

Were this suggestion well founded, it would follow that the intellectual difficulties of belief which we were considering earlier were misplaced. It would be a cardinal error to compare the plausibility of different world-views in an attempt to establish the reasonableness or unreasonableness of belief in God. For belief in God was not concerned with theoretical world-views at all. It did not set out to offer an explanation of the world. Rather, it announced a way of living in the world. There could, of course, be moral or psychological objections to this proposed way of life, that is, objections of a practical kind. But there could be no 'theoretical' objections. The only valid question for the would-be believer was whether or not to commit himself to this way of love. The question whether or not God 'in fact' existed was an unreal question. His 'existence' was not a question of fact, since it was necessarily presupposed by the way of self-abnegating love.

Such a point of view is, I believe, to be rejected. Without arguing the matter at length, I must simply affirm my own opinion that it fails to do justice to the theoretical and explanatory functions which belief in God has more commonly been thought to include, giving rise not only to a way of living in the world but also to a hope for man and the world. Belief in God is theory as well as practice, even if the theory cannot be fully understood apart from the practice. Nevertheless, there is a sense in which practice may well be allowed priority over theory. A person's fundamental orientation towards life, his openness in love towards his neighbour and the future, is reckoned by common sense to be of greater importance than the correctness of his theological beliefs. Common sense may underestimate the importance of belief in structuring and supporting the work of love. But its judgement cannot easily be gainsaid. Deeds speak louder than words, action than belief. To take the side of common sense at this point may sound to some to be subscribing to a very un-Christian doctrine of justification by works rather than by faith. If so, we may draw a measure of comfort by reminding ourselves that a former holder of the Chair of Moral and Pastoral Theology in this University, incomparably more distinguished than its present uneasy occupant, once dared to write: 'The sense in which I can say that I believe in the doctrine of justification by faith is, I fear, indistinguishable from what some people would call justification by works.'[5] In fact, it is not justification by works at all. It is justification by response. In Leonard Hodgson's own words: 'The faith which justifies is that fundamental faith which finds expression in a man's attempting to live up to the best light he has got, whether or no he has ever heard of the Christian gospel.'[6] The 'attempt' is a response to the 'light' which is given to him.

To commit oneself to the way of love is a moral choice. But the Christian proclamation is more than a summons to man to walk this way. It is also an affirmation that this way is the way of God in his world, that it is God's creative and redemptive initiative that prompts, sustains and will in the end fulfil man's pilgrimage along the way. Man's pilgrimage through time has its origin and destiny in eternity. But is this true? The Christian proclamation boldly declares that it is true. The Christian theologian endeavours to spell out in coherent doctrine *how* it may be true. What, however, of the half-believer? How does he stand? What may he with integrity believe and do?

The half-believer, disposed to follow the Christian way because he acknowledges in Jesus a manner of life which engages his deepest response, may, I suggest, without dishonesty act on the *assumption* that the basic Christian affirmation concerning the way of God is true. To assume that this affirmation is true is not the same thing as to believe that it is true. It is to accept it as a fundamental working hypothesis. In principle it is open to revision. Experience and further reflection may lead him at some future date to reject it. However, its truth or falsity cannot be tested by any isolated or nicely controlled experiment, nor by any clearly defined set of arguments. World-views cannot be tested in this way. For the experiment cannot be contained within a clearly defined context. It is an experiment with life.

This experiment may be initially justified for a number of reasons. For example, the way of love, expressed and exemplified in the teaching and life of Jesus, was itself in its original and concrete particularity the corollary of belief and trust in One whom Jesus called his heavenly Father. Belief and action formed an organic whole, action being the response to belief, belief evoking and supporting action. Jesus himself may be said to have experimented in this belief with his life; and although it seemed at first to everyone, including his disciples, that with his death on the cross his experiment had ended in failure, yet a few soon after his death and many down the ages have affirmed that out of his experiment has flowed a stream of grace and hope, revealing the experiment itself in a new and unexpected light. Death had indeed been overcome by life, fear by love. He in whom Jesus had trusted, apparently in vain, had continued to reveal himself as trustworthy, not despite the death of Jesus, but in and through his death. Jesus' experiment, therefore, to which he had called disciples, but which he had completed alone, needed now to be continued by his disciples.

Again, because the way of love is daunting and demanding, more than most men in their own strength can even dare to attempt, it is reasonable to test the claim that man's own love can be extended, deepened and renewed by a more than human love. A man needs to know not only what he is to do, but also the resources from which he may hope to receive. It is as much a fact of his human nature that he needs to belong as it is that he needs to be free. Were there a God, faithful and gracious, to whom he belonged, as a son to his father, the more free would he be to give himself to his neighbour

139

and to the world's future. His responsibility to his fellow-men would be sustained by his responsiveness to God. His human love would be rooted and grounded in the divine love. Surely, then, he is justified at least in making trial of God's love, in seeking communion with this mysterious Being in some of the various ways which believers have declared themselves to have experienced as means of grace.

Thus the half-believer may act on the assumption that the basic Christian affirmation concerning God is true. In so doing he commits himself to a way of life which claims his moral allegiance and assumes a belief which evokes, specifies and supports this way of life, a belief which, if true, confirms and validates it. He *assumes* this belief, but he does not *appropriate* it. It is the belief of others, it is not yet his own. For himself it remains more a hope than a belief, a hope with which he is determined to experiment in prayer, reflection and action, both as an individual and in the company of those who already believe. At times he feels he belongs to the community of belief, at other times that he does not belong. He is dependent on their understanding, patience and charity. So long as he remains a half-believer, his membership of the community of belief retains much of the character of his original movement towards it. The latter has been described by Gordon Kaufman in the following way:

> The decision is made on the basis of somewhat sketchy and fragmentary reports or intimations of the new possibilities that will open up, on the one hand, and because of dissatisfaction with the self's present situation, on the other. Like Abraham, the self moves away from its familiar environs, not really knowing into what kind of situation it is going (Heb.11:8). In such movements the self acts more on the basis of hope than knowledge. For hope

is that stance of the self toward a particular future which makes possible acceptance of its openness and unknown-ness as positive and inviting, rather than as so threatening or simply uninteresting as to forestall all movement towards it.[7]

The half-believer's experiment with life is intended, like Christian marriage, as an experiment for life, for nothing short of living and dying can provide an adequate and sufficient test. Like Christian marriage, however, the experiment may come to an untimely end. This may be due to a whole variety of causes and reasons. For example, courage, perseverance and even love may themselves grow cold. Or the community of faith, hope and charity, with which the half-believer links himself, may on better acquaintance appear to him as only another community of thinly disguised self-interest and self-protection. Or, again, further experience and reflection may lend greater, and in the end decisive, weight to the arguments for unbelief, thus showing his original commitment to have been misplaced. Conversion from belief to unbelief is as possible and as real as conversion from unbelief to belief.

On the other hand his experiment may lead to experiences which chime in with and tend to corroborate belief. Further reflection may afford a deeper understanding of belief, giving a greater range and coherence to its articulation in this or that theological form. Doubt is never finally dispelled, since no theology offers a satisfactory solution to all his intellectual problems. But assurance may increase. What was at the outset a belief which he assumed may imperceptibly develop into a belief that he has appropriated, his own belief. Nevertheless, because his belief is orientated towards creative future possibilities which present and past experience and reflection suggest but do not guarantee, so that he looks for the resurrection of the dead and the coming of God's kingdom finally to confirm the truth of his belief, if it is finally to be confirmed at all, belief and hope are difficult to distinguish. If it can be said that he 'believes' in God, it can also equally as well be said that he 'hopes' in God. And since in 'God' to be and to be trustworthy are necessarily one and the same thing, God's existence is as much the object of his believing hope as is God's trustworthiness. To put the matter paradoxically, we may say that he trusts God to exist!

For the half-believer the question of God remains, at the intellectual level, a persistently open question. The accounts cannot finally be settled or the books shut. When, then, he commits himself to the Christian life in faith and hope, he confesses at the same time to a dividedness within himself which refuses to be healed. Justified through faith he may be, but he is not yet made whole in faith. Doubt is not done away. Is this undercurrent of doubt a symptom of his estrangement from God and his lack of love? Or may it also be a sign that his wholeness must wait upon the wholeness of his neighbour, even of creation itself? Dare he even hope—for such indeed is his prayer—that his expectant but troubled half-belief, his experiment with life in love, an experiment which he finds himself unable either to give up or to complete, may itself minister grace to others who also find belief in God an inviting but disturbing enterprise? If he may so dare, then he will rejoice in his heart, praising and glorifying him in whom he believes and does not believe.

NOTES

Chapter 1: Appeal to experience

1 I regret that I have been unable to trace this quotation to its source.
2 E. E. Hirschmann, *On Human Unity* (Victor Gollancz, 1961), p. 198.
3 D. H. Mellor, 'Religious and secular statements', *Philosophy*, January 1974, p. 41.
4 John Hick, *Faith and Knowledge* (Macmillan, 1967), p. 53.
5 *Ibid.*, p. 209.
6 For a detailed treatment of this point, see B. Mitchell, *The Justification of Religious Belief* (Macmillan, 1973), chap. 6.
7 From A. H. Maslow, *Religions, Values and Peak-Experiences* (Ohio State University Press, 1964); quoted in *Personality and Religion*, ed. William A. Sadler, Jnr (SCM, 1970), p. 169.
8 D. H. Mellor, *op. cit.*, p. 41.
9 Langdon Gilkey, *Naming the Whirlwind* (Bobbs-Merrill, 1969), p. 269.

Chapter 2: The Question of Man

1 Maurice Friedman, *To Deny Our Nothingness* (Victor Gollancz, 1967), p. 358f.
2 *The Times*, 9 January 1974.
3 Langdon Gilkey, *Religion and the Scientific Future* (SCM, 1970), p. 82.
4 Michael Novak, *The Experience of Nothingness* (Harper & Row, 1970), chap. 2.

5 For a summary of his 'transcendental method', see Bernard Lonergan, *Method in Theology* (Darton, Longman & Todd, 1972), chap. 1.

6 R. W. Hepburn, 'Method and insight', *Philosophy*, April 1973, p. 158.

7 Schubert Ogden, *The Reality of God* (SCM, 1967), p. 36.

8 *Ibid.*, p. 37.

9 Langdon Gilkey, *Naming the Whirlwind* (Bobbs-Merrill, 1969), p. 296.

10 Roger Garaudy, *From Anathema to Dialogue* (Collins, 1967), p. 80.

11 See Peter L. Berger, *A Rumour of Angels* (Allen Lane, 1969).

Chapter 3: Interim Faith?

1 Nathan A. Scott, Jnr, *Negative Capability* (Yale University Press, 1969), p. 75. The quotations are from Gerard Manley Hopkins.

2 Roger Garaudy, 'Faith and revolution', *The Ecumenical Review*, January 1973, p. 64.

3 *Ibid.*, p. 65.

4 J. Bronowski, *Science and Human Values*; quoted in Paul Ramsey, *Fabricated Man* (Yale University Press, 1970), p. 21.

5 I should like to acknowledge my indebtedness here to that sensitive and profound book by John S. Dunne, *The Way of All the Earth* (Sheldon Press, 1973).

Chapter 4: Grounds for Hope

1 A. O. Dyson, *The Immortality of the Past* (SCM, 1974), p. 73.

2 Ps. 115.1.

3 Rubem Alves, *A Theology of Human Hope* (Corpus Books, 1969), p. 13f.

4 J. P. van Praag, in *A Catholic–Humanist Dialogue*, ed. by Paul Kurtz and Albert Dondeyne (Pemberton Books, 1972), p. 6.

5 Van Praag, *op. cit.*, p. 5.

6 V. A. Demant, 'Humanism, Christian and secularist', *Theology*, June 1973, p. 303.

7 Iris Murdoch, *The Sovereignty of Good* (Routledge & Kegan

Paul, 1970), p. 83.

8 Henry McKeating, *Living with Guilt* (SCM, 1970), p. 78.

9 K. Britton, *Philosophy and the Meaning of Life* (Cambridge University Press, 1969), p. 215.

10 *Gaudium et Spes,* 41.

11 Van Praag, *op. cit.*, p. 7f.

12 Ps. 139.7, 11 (*Book of Common Prayer*).

13 Nathan A. Scott, Jnr, *Negative Capability* (Yale University Press, 1969), p. 159.

Chapter 5. The Way of Jesus

1 J. L. Houlden, *Ethics and the New Testament* (Penguin Books, 1973), p. 104f.

2 Mark 10.5 (*NEB*). The older translation of the Greek word is 'hardness of heart'.

3 I take it that, although Jesus was sentenced to death by the political authorities, it was not in fact a political, but rather a religious, offence which led to his execution.

4 Kurt Niederwimmer, *Jesus*; quoted in J. L. Houlden, *op. cit.*, p. 111. Houlden's whole chapter merits careful reading.

5 See Henry McKeating, *Living with Guilt* (SCM, 1970).

6 *Ibid.,* p. 117f.

7 *Ibid.*, p. 107.

8 For a fuller discussion of the strengths and weaknesses of this approach, see Gene Outka, *Agape* (Yale University Press, 1972), chap. 6, *passim*.

9 For a more detailed exploration of this approach, see C. D. Batson, J. C. Becker and W. M. Clark, *Commitment without Ideology* (SCM, 1973).

10 Batson, Becker and Clark, *op. cit.,* p. 69.

11 H. A. Williams, *True Resurrection* (Mitchell Beazley, 1972), p. 175f.

12 Batson, Becker and Clark, *op. cit.,* p. 184.

13 Van A. Harvey, 'Secularism, responsible belief and the "Theology of Hope"', *The Future of Hope,* ed. Frederick Herzog (Herder & Herder, 1970), p. 150f.

Chapter 6: The Kingdom of God

1 See p. 88.
2 Langdon Gilkey, *Naming the Whirlwind* (Bobbs-Merrill, 1969), p. 354f.
3 Frank Kermode, *The Sense of an Ending* (Oxford University Press, 1968), p. 35.
4 Paul Ramsey, *Fabricated Man* (Yale University Press, 1970), p. 27.
5 Lenin; quoted by Roger Garaudy, 'Faith and revolution', *The Ecumenical Review*, January 1973, p. 63.
6 In the following reflections I wish to acknowledge a special debt to D. Cupitt's *Christ and the Hiddenness of God*, as well as to the correspondence between Cupitt and C. F. D. Moule in *Theology*, October 1972; also to Robert W. Jenson, *The Knowledge of Things Hoped For* (Oxford University Press, N.Y., 1969), p. 224f.
7 Robert W. Jenson, *op. cit.,* p. 228.
8 Gal. 3.13.
9 1 Pet. 1.3.
10 Rudolf Bultmann, *History and Eschatology* (Edinburgh University Press, 1957), p. 151.
11 *Ibid.,* p. 153.
12 J. Macquarrie, 'Eschatology and Time', in *The Future of Hope,* ed. F. Herzog (Herder & Herder, 1970), p. 125.
13 James F. Gustafson, *Christian Ethics and the Community* (Pilgrim Press, 1971), p. 210.
14 John Donne, from a sermon delivered at Whitehall on 29 February 1627/8.

Chapter 7: Presence and Promise

1 Dom Aelred Graham, *The End of Religion* (Harcourt Brace Jovanovich, 1971), p. 80.
2 *Ibid.,* p. 239.
3 1 Thess. 5.24.
4 John Macquarrie, *op. cit.*, p. 117. This whole essay contains a highly sensitive and perceptive discussion of the significance of eschatological imagery.
5 Rudolf Bultmann, *History and Eschatology* (Edinburgh

University Press, 1957), p. 151f.

6 *Ibid.*, p. 155.
7 Quoted in William A. Beardslee, *A House for Hope* (Westminster Press, 1972), p. 17.
8 C. S. Lewis, *Letters to Malcolm* (Geoffrey Bles, 1964), p. 121f.
9 From A. H. Maslow, *Religions, Values and Peak-Experiences* (Ohio State University Press, 1964). Compiled and quoted in *Personality and Religion,* ed. William A. Sadler, Jnr (SCM, 1970), p. 171f.
10 Compare and contrast the view, put forward by Ninian Smart (e.g. in *The Yogi and the Devotee*) that there are *two* basic types of religious experience: the mystical and the prophetic, each of which tends towards a different interpretative world-view.
11 Maslow, *op. cit.*, p. 178.
12 *Ibid.*, p. 179.
13 Beardslee, *op. cit.*, p. 37.
14 John Passmore, *The Perfectibility of Man* (Duckworth, 1970), p. 302.
15 E.g. Sri Aurobindo. For a brief account of Auribindo's attempt to harmonise time and eternity in an 'integral' philosophy, see Jehangir N. Chubb, 'Sri Aurobindo as the fulfilment of Hinduism', *International Philosophical Quarterly,* June 1972.
16 Passmore, *op. cit.*, p. 295.
17 Gabriel Marcel, *The Mystery of Being*, vol. 2 (Harvill Press, 1951), p. 153.
18 Beardslee, *op. cit.*, p. 109.
19 J. E. Fison, *The Christian Hope* (Longmans, Green & Co., 1954), p. 50.

Chapter 8: Experiment with Life

1 Oliver Cromwell, 'Letter to the General Assembly of the Church of Scotland', 3 August 1650.
2 1 Cor. 13.4–6 (*NEB*).
3 D. Z. Phillips, 'Faith, scepticism and religious understanding', in *Religion and Understanding*, ed. D. Z. Phillips (Blackwell, 1967), p. 74. Phillips is here elaborating on the thought of S. Kierkegaard in his *Works of Love*.

NOTES

4 Phillips, *op. cit.*, p. 75.
5 Leonard Hodgson, *For Faith and Freedom* (Blackwell, 1956), vol. I, p. 109.
6 *Ibid.,* p. 109.
7 Gordon D. Kaufman, *God the Problem* (Harvard University Press, 1972), p. 245.